Ex Libris

A Good Book is the precious life blood of a master spirit embalmed and treasured up on purpose to a life beyond life.

Milton.

In memory of
Carrie Gibboney Grimsley

LETTERS

LETTERS

ON THE

EQUALITY OF THE SEXES

AND THE

CONDITION OF WOMAN

By Sarah M. Grimké

SOURCE BOOK PRESS

HQ
1423
.G8
1970b

All rights reserved. No part of this book may be reproduced
in any form without permission from the publisher.
Library of Congress Catalogue Card No. 71-134189
ISBN 0-87681-061-X
SOURCE BOOK PRESS, a Division of Collectors Editions Ltd.,
185 Madison Avenue, New York, N.Y. 10016
Unabridged republication of the 1838 Boston edition: First printing 1970
Reprinted from a copy in the collections of the Harvard College Library
Manufactured in the United States of America

DABNEY LANCASTER LIBRARY
LONGWOOD COLLEGE
FARMVILLE, VIRGINIA 23901

LETTERS

ON THE

EQUALITY OF THE SEXES,

AND THE

CONDITION OF WOMAN.

ADDRESSED TO

MARY S. PARKER,

PRESIDENT OF THE

Boston Female Anti-Slavery Society.

———

BOSTON:
PUBLISHED BY ISAAC KNAPP,
25, CORNHILL.

———

1838.

71-05016

LETTERS.

LETTER I.

THE ORIGINAL EQUALITY OF WOMAN.

Amesbury, 7th Mo. 11th, 1837.

MY DEAR FRIEND,—In attempting to comply with thy request to give my views on the Province of Woman, I feel that I am venturing on nearly untrodden ground, and that I shall advance arguments in opposition to a corrupt public opinion, and to the perverted interpretation of Holy Writ, which has so universally obtained. But I am in search of truth; and no obstacle shall prevent my prosecuting that search, because I believe the welfare of the world will be materially advanced by every new discovery we make of the designs of Jehovah in the creation of woman. It is impossible that we can answer the purpose of our being, unless we understand that purpose. It is impossible that we should fulfil our duties, unless we comprehend them; or live up to our privileges, unless we know what they are.

In examining this important subject, I shall depend solely on the Bible to designate the sphere of woman, because I believe almost every thing that has been written on this subject, has been the result of a misconception of the simple truths revealed in the Scriptures, in consequence of the false translation of many passages of Holy Writ. My mind is entirely delivered from the superstitious reverence which is attached to the English version of the Bible. King James's translators certainly were not inspired. I therefore claim the original as my standard, *believing that to have been inspired*, and I also claim to judge for myself what is the meaning of the inspired writers, because I believe it to be the solemn duty of every individual to search the Scriptures for themselves, with the aid of the Holy Spirit, and not be governed by the views of any man, or set of men.

We must first view woman at the period of her creation. 'And God said, Let us make man in our own image, after our likeness; and let them have dominion over the fish of the sea, and over the fowl of the air, and over the cattle, and over all the earth, and over every creeping thing that creepeth upon the earth. So God created man in his own image, in the image of God created he him, male and female created he them.' In all this sublime description of the creation of man, (which is a generic term including man and woman,) there is not one particle of difference intimated as existing between them. They were both made in the image of God; dominion was given to both over every other creature, but not over each other. Created in perfect equality, they were expected to exercise the vicegerence intrusted to them by their Maker, in harmony and love.

Let us pass on now to the recapitulation of the creation of man —'The Lord God formed man of the dust of the ground, and breathed into his nostrils the breath of life; and man became a living soul. And the Lord God said, it is not good that man should be alone, I will make him an help meet for him.' All creation swarmed with animated beings capable of natural affection, as we know they still are; it was not, therefore, merely to give man a creature susceptible of loving, obeying, and looking up to him, for all that the animals could do and did do. It was to give him a companion, *in all respects* his equal; one who was like himself *a free agent*, gifted with intellect and endowed with immortality; not a partaker merely of his animal gratifications, but able to enter into all his feelings as a moral and responsible being. If this had not been the case, how could she have been an help meet for him? I understand this as applying not only to the parties entering into the marriage contract, but to all men and women, because I believe God designed woman to be an help meet for man in every good and perfect work. She was a part of himself, as if Jehovah designed to make the oneness and identity of man and woman perfect and complete; and when the glorious work of their creation was finished, 'the morning stars sang together, and all the sons of God shouted for joy.'

This blissful condition was not long enjoyed by our first parents. Eve, it would seem from the history, was wandering alone amid the bowers of Paradise, when the serpent

met with her. From her reply to Satan, it is
evident that the command not to eat 'of the
tree that is in the midst of the garden,' was
given to both, although the term man was used
when the prohibition was issued by God.
'And the woman said unto the serpent, WE may
eat of the fruit of the trees of the garden, but
of the fruit of the tree which is in the midst of
the garden, God hath said, YE shall not eat of
it, neither shall YE touch it, lest YE die.' Here
the woman was exposed to temptation from a
being with whom she was unacquainted. She
had been accustomed to associate with her beloved partner, and to hold communion with God
and with angels; but of satanic intelligence,
she was in all probability entirely ignorant.
Through the subtlety of the serpent, she was
beguiled. And 'when she saw that the tree
was good for food, and that it was pleasant to
the eyes, and a tree to be desired to make one
wise, she took of the fruit thereof and did eat.'

We next find Adam involved in the same
sin, not through the instrumentality of a supernatural agent, but through that of his equal, a
being whom he must have known was liable to
transgress the divine command, because he
must have felt that he was himself a free agent,
and that he was restrained from disobedience
only by the exercise of faith and love towards
his Creator. Had Adam tenderly reproved his
wife, and endeavored to lead her to repentance
instead of sharing in her guilt, I should be
much more ready to accord to man that superiority which he claims; but as the facts stand
disclosed by the sacred historian, it appears to
me that to say the least, there was as much
weakness exhibited by Adam as by Eve.

They both fell from innocence, and consequently from happiness, *but not from equality*.

Let us next examine the conduct of this fallen pair, when Jehovah interrogated them respecting their fault. Thy both frankly confessed their guilt. 'The man said, the woman whom thou gavest to be with me, she gave me of the tree and I did eat. And the woman said, the serpent beguiled me and I did eat.' And the Lord God said unto the woman, 'Thou wilt be subject unto thy husband, and he will rule over thee.' That this did not allude to the subjection of woman to man is manifest, because the same mode of expression is used in speaking to Cain of Abel. The truth is that the curse, as it is termed, which was pronounced by Jehovah upon woman, is a simple prophecy. The Hebrew, like the French language, uses the same word to express shall and will. Our translators having been accustomed to exercise lordship over their wives, and seeing only through the medium of a perverted judgment, very naturally, though I think not very learnedly or very kindly, translated it *shall* instead of *will*, and thus converted a prediction to Eve into a command to Adam; for observe, it is addressed to the woman and not to the man. The consequence of the fall was an immediate struggle for dominion, and Jehovah foretold which would gain the ascendency; but as he created them in his image, as that image manifestly was not lost by the fall, because it is urged in Gen. 9:6, as an argument why the life of man should not be taken by his fellow man, there is no reason to suppose that sin produced any distinction between them as moral, intellectual and responsible beings. Man might just as well have endeavored by hard labor to fulfil the prophecy, thorns and thistles will the earth bring forth to thee, as to pretend to accomplish the other, 'he will rule over thee,' by asserting dominion over his wife.

> 'Authority usurped from God, not given.
> He gave him only over beast, flesh, flowl,
> Dominion absolute: that right he holds
> By God's donation: but man o'er woman
> He made not Lord, such title to himself
> Reserving, human left from human free.'

Here then I plant myself. God created us equal;—he created us free agents;—he is our Lawgiver, our King and our Judge, and to him alone is woman bound to be in subjection, and to him alone is she accountable for the use of those talents with which her Heavenly Father has entrusted her. One is her Master even Christ.

Thine for the oppressed in the bonds of woman hood, SARAH M. GRIMKE.

LETTER II.

Newburyport, 7th mo. 17, 1837.

MY DEAR SISTER,—In my last, I traced the
creation and the fall of man and woman from
that state of purity and happiness which their
beneficent Creator designed them to enjoy. As
they were one in transgression, their chastisement was the same. 'So God drove out *the
man,* and he placed at the East of the garden
of Eden a cherubim and a flaming sword, which
turned every way to keep the way of the tree
of life.' We now behold them expelled from
Paradise, fallen from their original loveliness, but
still bearing on their foreheads the image and
superscription of Jehovah; still invested with
high moral responsibilites, intellectual powers,
and immortal souls. They had incurred the
penalty of sin, they were shorn of their innocence, but they stood on the same platform side
by side, acknowledging *no superior* but their
God. Notwithstanding what has been urged,
woman I am aware stands charged to the present day with having brought sin into the world.
I shall not repel the charge by any counter
assertions, although, as was before hinted, Adam's ready acquiescence with his wife's propo-

sal, does not savor much of that superiority *in strength of mind*, which is arrogated by man. Even admitting that Eve was the greater sinner, it seems to me man might be satisfied with the dominion he has claimed and exercised for nearly six thousand years, and that more true nobility would be manifested by endeavoring to raise the fallen and invigorate the weak, than by keeping woman in subjection. But I ask no favors for my sex. I surrender not our claim to equality. All I ask of our brethren is, that they will take their feet from off our necks, and permit us to stand upright on that ground which God designed us to occupy. If he has not given us the rights which have, as I conceive, been wrested from us, we shall soon give evidence of our inferiority, and shrink back into that obscurity, which the high souled magnanimity of man has assigned us as our appropriate sphere.

As I am unable to learn from sacred writ when woman was deprived by God of her equality with man, I shall touch upon a few points in the Scriptures, which demonstrate that no supremacy was granted to man. When God had destroyed the world, except Noah and his family, by the deluge, he renewed the grant formerly made to man, and again gave him dominion over every beast of the earth, every fowl of the air, over all that moveth upon the earth, and over all the fishes of the sea; into his hands they were delivered. But was woman, bearing the image of her God, placed under the dominion of her fellow man? Never! Jehovah could not surrender his authority to govern his own immortal creatures into the hands of a being, whom he knew, and whom his

whole history proved, to be unworthy of a trust
so sacred and important. God could not do it,
because it is a direct contravention of his law,
' Thou shalt worship the Lord thy God, and *him
only* shalt thou serve.' If Jehovah had appointed man as the guardian, or teacher of woman,
he would certainly have given some intimation
of this surrender of his own prerogative. But
so far from it, we find the commands of God
invariably the same to man and woman ; and
not the slightest intimation is given in a single
passage of the Bible, that God designed to
point woman to man as her instructor. The
tenor of his language always is, ' Look unto
ME, and be ye saved, all the ends of the earth,
for I am God, and there is none else.'

The lust of dominion was probably the first
effect of the fall; and as there was no other
intelligent being over whom to exercise it, woman was the first victim of this unhallowed passion. We afterwards see it exhibited by Cain
in the murder of his brother, by Nimrod in his
becoming a mighty hunter of men, and setting
up a kingdom over which to reign. Here we
see the origin of that Upas of slavery, which
sprang up immediately after the fall, and has
spread its pestilential branches over the whole
face of the known world. All history attests
that man has subjected woman to his will, used
her as a means to promote his selfish gratification, to minister to his sensual pleasures, to be
instrumental in promoting his comfort; but
never has he desired to elevate her to that rank
she was created to fill. He has done all he
could to debase and enslave her mind; and
now he looks triumphantly on the ruin he has
wrought, and says, the being he has thus deeply
injured is his inferior.

Woman has been placed by John Quincy Adams, side by side with the slave, whilst he was contending for the right side of petition. I thank him for ranking us with the oppressed; for I shall not find it difficult to show, that in all ages and countries, not even excepting enlightened republican America, woman has more or less been made a *means* to promote the welfare of man, without due regard to her own happiness, and the glory of God as the end of her creation.

During the *patriarchal* ages, we find men and women engaged in the same employments. Abraham and Sarah both assisted in preparing the food which was to be set before the three men, who visited them in the plains of Mamre; but although their occupations were similar, Sarah was not permitted to enjoy the society of the holy visitant; and as we learn from Peter, that she 'obeyed Abraham, calling him Lord,' we may presume he exercised dominion over her. We shall pass on now to Rebecca. In her history, we find another striking illustration of the low estimation in which woman was held. Eleazur is sent to seek a wife for Isaac. He finds Rebecca going down to the well to fill her pitcher. He accosts her; and she replies with all humility, 'Drink, my lord.' How does he endeavor to gain her favor and confidence? Does he approach her as a dignified creature, whom he was about to invite to fill an important station in his master's family, as the wife of his only son? No. He offered incense to her vanity, and 'he took a golden ear-ring of half a shekel weight, and two bracelets for her hands of ten shekels weight of gold,' and gave them to Rebecca.

The cupidity of man soon led him to regard woman as property, and hence we find them sold to those, who wished to marry them, as far as appears, without any regard to those sacred rights which belong to woman, as well as to man in the choice of a companion. That women were a profitable kind of property, we may gather from the description of a virtuous woman int he last chapter of Proverbs. To work willingly with her hands, to open her hands to the poor, to clothe herself with silk and purple, to look well to her household, to make fine linen and sell it, to deliver girdles to the merchant, and not to eat the bread of idleness, seems to have constituted in the view of Solomon, the perfection of a woman's character and achievements. 'The spirit of that age was not favorable to intellectual improvement; but as there were wise men who formed exceptions to the general ignorance, and were destined to guide the world into more advanced states, so there was a corresponding proportion of wise women; and among the Jews, as well as other nations, we find a strong tendency to believe that women were in more immediate connection with heaven than men.'—L. M. Child's Con. of Woman. If there be any truth in this tradition, I am at a loss to imagine in what the superiority of man consists.

Thine in the bonds of womanhood,

SARAH M. GRIMKE.

LETTER III.

Haverhill, 7th Mo. 1837.

DEAR FRIEND,—When I last addressed thee,
I had not seen the Pastoral Letter of the General Association. It has since fallen into my
hands, and I must digress from my intention of
exhibiting the condition of women in different
parts of the world, in order to make some remarks on this extraordinary document. I am
persuaded that when the minds of men and
women become emancipated from the thraldom
of superstition and ' traditions of men,' the sentiments contained in the Pastoral Letter will be
recurred to with as much astonishment as the
opinions of Cotton Mather and other distinguished men of his day, on the subject of witchcraft; nor will it be deemed less wonderful,
that a body of divines should gravely assemble
and endeavor to prove that woman has no right
to ' open her mouth for the dumb,' than it now
is that judges should have sat on the trials of
witches, and solemnly condemned nineteen persons and one dog to death for witchcraft.

But to the letter. It says, ' We invite your

attention to the dangers which at present seem to threaten the FEMALE CHARACTER with wide-spread and permanent injury.' I rejoice that they have called the attention of my sex to this subject, because I believe if woman investigates it, she will soon discover that danger is impending, though from a totally different source from that which the Association apprehends,—danger from those who, having long held the reins of *usurped* authority, are unwilling to permit us to fill that sphere which God created us to move in, and who have entered into league to crush the immortal mind of woman. I rejoice, because I am persuaded that the rights of woman, like the rights of slaves, need only be examined to be understood and asserted, even by some of those, who are now endeavoring to smother the irrepressible desire for mental and spiritual freedom which glows in the breast of many, who hardly dare to speak their sentiments.

'The appropriate duties and influence of women are clearly stated in the New Testament. Those duties are unobtrusive and private, but the sources of *mighty power*. When the mild, *dependent*, softening influence of woman upon the sternness of man's opinions is fully exercised, society feels the effects of it in a thousand ways.' No one can desire more earnestly than I do, that woman may move exactly in the sphere which her Creator has assigned her; and I believe her having been displaced from that sphere has introduced confusion into the world. It is, therefore, of vast importance to herself and to all the rational creation, that she should ascertain what are her duties and her privileges as a responsible and immortal being.

The New Testament has been referred to, and I am willing to abide by its decisions, but must enter my protest against the false translation of some passages by the MEN who did that work, and against the perverted interpretation by the MEN who undertook to write commentaries thereon. I am inclined to think, when we are admitted to the honor of studying Greek and Hebrew, we shall produce some various readings of the Bible a little different from those we now have.

The Lord Jesus defines the duties of his followers in his Sermon on the Mount. He lays down grand principles by which they should be governed, without any reference to sex or condition .—' Ye are the light of the world. A city that is set on a hill cannot be hid. Neither do men light a candle and put it under a bushel, but on a candlestick, and it giveth light unto all that are in the house. Let your light so shine before men, that they may see your good works, and glorify your Father which is in Heaven.' I follow him through all his precepts, and find him giving the same directions to women as to men, never even referring to the distinction now so strenuously insisted upon between masculine and feminine virtues : this is one of the anti-christian ' traditions of men' which are taught instead of the ' commandments of God.' Men and women were CREATED EQUAL ; they are both moral and accountable beings, and whatever is *right* for man to do, is *right* for woman.

But the influence of woman, says the Association, is to be private and unobtrusive ; her light is not to shine before man like that of her brethren ; but she is passively to let the lords

of the creation, as they call themselves, put the
bushel over it, lest peradventure it might appear
that the world has been benefitted by the rays
of *her* candle.   So that her quenched light, according to their judgment, will be of more use
than if it were set on the candlestick.   'Her
influence is the source of mighty power.'   This
has ever been the flattering language of man
since he laid aside the whip as a means to keep
woman in subjection.   He spares her body; but
the war he has waged against her mind, her
heart, and her soul, has been no less destructive
to her as a moral being.   How monstrous, how
anti-christian, is the doctrine that woman is to
be dependent on man!   Where, in all the sacred
Scriptures, is this taught?   Alas! she has too
well learned the lesson which MAN has labored
to teach her.   She has surrendered her dearest
RIGHTS, and been satisfied with the privileges
which man has assumed to grant her; she
has been amused with the show of power, whilst
man has absorbed all the reality into himself.
He has adorned the creature whom God gave
him as a companion, with baubles and gewgaws,
turned her attention to personal attractions,
offered incense to her vanity, and made her the
instrument of his selfish gratification, a play-
thing to please his eye and amuse his hours of
leisure.   'Rule by obedience and by submission
sway,' or in other words, study to be a hypo-
crite, pretend to submit, but gain your point,
has been the code of household morality which
woman has been taught.   The poet has sung,
in sickly strains, the loveliness of woman's dependence upon man, and now we find it re-
echoed by those who profess to teach the religion of the Bible.   God says, 'Cease ye from

man whose breath is in his nostrils, for wherein
is he to be accounted of?' Man says, depend
upon me. God says, ' HE will teach us of his
ways.' Man says, believe it not, I am to be
your teacher. This doctrine of dependence
upon man is utterly at variance with the doctrine of the Bible. In that book I find nothing
like the softness of woman, nor the sternness of
man : both are equally commanded to bring
forth the fruits of the Spirit, love, meekness,
gentleness, &c.

But we are told, 'the power of woman is in
her dependence, flowing from a consciousness
of that weakness which God has given her for
her protection.' If physical weakness is allu-
ded to, I cheerfully concede the superiority ; if
brute force is what my brethren are claiming, I
am willing to let them have all the honor they
desire ; but if they mean to intimate, that mental or moral weakness belongs to woman, more
than to man, I utterly disclaim the charge. Our
powers of mind have been crushed, as far as
man could do it, our sense of morality has
been impaired by his interpretation of our duties ; but no where does God say that he made
any distinction between us, as moral and intelligent beings.

' We appreciate,' say the Association, 'the
unostentatious prayers and efforts of woman in
advancing the cause of religion at home and
abroad, in leading religious inquirers TO THE
PASTOR for instruction.' Several points here
demand attention. If public prayers and public
efforts are necessarily ostentatious, then ' Anna
the prophetess, (or preacher,) who departed not
from the temple, but served God with fastings
and prayers night and day,' 'and spake of

Christ to all them that looked for redemption in
Israel,' was ostentatious in her efforts. Then,
the apostle Paul encourages women to be ostentatious in their efforts to spread the gospel,
when he gives them directions how they should
appear, when engaged in praying, or preaching
in the public assemblies. Then, the whole association of Congregational ministers are ostentatious, in the efforts they are making in preaching and praying to convert souls.

But woman may be permitted to lead religious inquirers to the PASTORS for instruction.
Now this is assuming that all pastors are better
qualified to give instruction than woman. This
I utterly deny. I have suffered too keenly from
the teaching of man, to lead any one to him for
instruction. The Lord Jesus says,—' Come
unto me and learn of me.' He points his followers to no man; and when woman is made
the favored instrument of rousing a sinner to
his lost and helpless condition, she has no right
to substitute any teacher for Christ; all she has
to do is, to turn the contrite inquirer to the
' Lamb of God which taketh away the sins of
the world.' More souls have probably been
lost by going down to Egypt for help, and by
trusting in man in the early stages of religious
experience, than by any other error. Instead of
the petition being offered to God,—' Lead me
in thy truth, and TEACH me, for thou art the
God of my salvation,'—instead of relying on the
precious promises—' What man is he that fear-
eth the Lord? him shall HE TEACH in the way
that he shall choose'—' I will instruct thee and
TEACH thee in the way which thou shalt go—I
will guide thee with mine eye'—the young
convert is directed to go to man, as if he were

in the place of God, and his instructions essential to an advancement in the path of righteousness. That woman can have but a poor conception of the privilege of being taught of God, what he alone can teach, who would turn the 'religious inquirer aside' from the fountain of living waters, where he might slake his thirst for spiritual instruction, to those broken cisterns which can hold no water, and therefore cannot satisfy the panting spirit. The business of men and women, who are ORDAINED OF GOD to preach the unsearchable riches of Christ' to a lost and perishing world, is to lead souls to Christ, and not to Pastors for instruction.

The General Association say, that 'when woman assumes the place and tone of man as a public reformer, our care and protection of her seem unnecessary; we put ourselves in self-defence against her, and her character becomes unnatural.' Here again the unscriptural notion is held up, that there is a distinction between the duties of men and women as moral beings; that what is virtue in man, is vice in woman; and women who dare to obey the command of Jehovah, 'Cry aloud, spare not, lift up thy voice like a trumpet, and show my people their transgression,' are threatened with having the protection of the brethren withdrawn. If this is all they do, we shall not even know the time when our chastisement is inflicted; our trust is in the Lord Jehovah, and in him is everlasting strength. The motto of woman, when she is engaged in the great work of public reformation should be,—'The Lord is my light and my salvation; whom shall I fear? The Lord is the strength of my life; of whom shall I be afraid?' She must feel, if she feels rightly, that she is fulfilling one of the important duties laid upon her as an accountable being, and that her character, instead of being 'unnatural,' is in exact accordance with the will of Him to whom, and to no other, she is responsible for the talents and the gifts confided to her. As to the pretty simile, introduced into the 'Pastoral Lerter,' 'If the vine whose strength and beauty is to lean upon the trellis work, and half conceal its clusters, thinks to assume the independence and the overshadowing nature of the elm,' &c. I shall only remark that it might well suit the poet's fancy, who sings of sparkling eyes and coral lips, and knights in armor clad ; but it seems to me utterly inconsistent with the dignity of a Christian body, to endeavor to draw such an anti-scriptural distinction between men and women. Ah! how many of my sex feel in the dominion, thus unrighteously exercised over them, under the gentle appellation of *protection*, that what they have leaned upon has proved a broken reed at best, and oft a spear.

Thine in the bonds of womanhood,

SARAH M. GRIMKE.

LETTER IV.

Andover, 7th Mo. 27th, 1837.

MY DEAR FRIEND,—Before I proceed with the account of that oppression which woman has suffered in every age and country from her *protector*, man, permit me to offer for your consideration, some views relative to the social intercourse of the sexes. Nearly the whole of this intercourse is, in my apprehension, derogatory to man and woman, as moral and intellectual beings. We approach each other, and mingle with each other, under the constant pressure of a feeling that we are of different sexes; and, instead of regarding each other only in the light of immortal creatures, the mind is fettered by the idea which is early and industriously infused into it, that we must never forget the distinction between male and female. Hence our intercourse, instead of being elevated and refined, is generally calculated to excite and keep alive the lowest propensities of our nature. Nothing, I believe, has tended more to destroy the true dignity of woman, than the fact that she is approached by man in the character of a female. The idea that she is sought as an intelligent and heaven-born creature, whose so-

ciety will cheer, refine and elevate her companion, and that she will receive the same blessings
she confers, is rarely held up to her view. On
the contrary, man almost always addresses
himself to the weakness of woman. By flattery, by an appeal to her passions, he seeks
access to her heart; and when he has gained her affections, he uses her as the instrument
of his pleasure—the minister of his temporal
comfort. He furnishes himself with a housekeeper, whose chief business is in the kitchen,
or the nursery. And whilst he goes abroad
and enjoys the means of improvement afforded
by collision of intellect with cultivated minds,
his wife is condemned to draw nearly all her
instruction from books, if she has time to pe-
ruse them; and if not, from her meditations,
whilst engaged in those domestic duties, which
are necessary for the comfort of her lord and
master.

Surely no one who contemplates, with the
eye of a Christian philosopher, the design of
God in the creation of woman, can believe that
she is now fulfilling that design. The literal
translation of the word 'help-meet' is a helper like unto himself; it is so rendered in the
Septuagint, and manifestly signifies a companion. Now I believe it will be impossible for
woman to fill the station assigned her by God,
until her brethren mingle with her as an equal,
as a moral being; and lose, in the dignity of
her immortal nature, and in the fact of her bearing like himself the image and superscription
of her God, the idea of her being a female.
The apostle beautifully remarks, 'As many of
you as have been baptized into Christ, have put
on Christ. There is neither Jew nor Greek,

there is neither bond nor free, there is neither *male* nor *female ;* for ye are all one in Christ Jesus.' Until our intercourse is purified by the forgetfulness of sex,—until we rise above the present low and sordid views which entwine themselves around our social and domestic interchange of sentiment and feelings, we never can derive that benefit from each other's society which it is the design of our Creator that we should. Man has inflicted an unspeakable injury upon woman, by holding up to her view her animal nature, and placing in the back ground her moral and intellectual being. Woman has inflicted an injury upon herself by submitting to be thus regarded ; and she is now called upon to rise from the station where *man*, not God, has placed her, and claim those sacred and inalienable rights, as a moral and responsible being, with which her Creator has invested her.

What but these views, so derogatory to the character of woman, could have called forth the remark contained in the Pastoral Letter ? ' We especially deplore the intimate acquaintance and promiscuous conversation of *females* with regard to things " which ought not to be named," by which that modesty and delicacy, which is the charm of domestic life, and which constitutes the true influence of woman, is consumed.' How wonderful that the conceptions of man relative to woman are so low, that he cannot perceive that she may converse on any subject connected with the improvement of her species, without swerving in the least from that modesty which is one of her greatest virtues ! Is it designed to insinuate that woman should possess a greater degree of modesty than man ?

This idea I utterly reprobate. Or is it supposed that woman cannot go into scenes of misery, the necessary result of those very things, which the Pastoral Letter says ought not to be named, for the purpose of moral reform, without becoming contaminated by those with whom she thus mingles?

This is a false position; and I presume has grown out of the never-forgotten distinction of male and female. The woman who goes forth, clad in the panoply of God, to stem the tide of iniquity and misery, which she beholds rolling through our land, goes not forth to her labor of love as a female. She goes as the dignified messenger of Jehevah, and all she does and says must be done and said irrespective of sex. She is in duty bound to communicate with all, who are able and willing to aid her in saving her fellow creatures, both men and women, from that destruction which awaits them.

So far from woman losing any thing of the purity of her mind, by visiting the wretched victims of vice in their miserable abodes, by talking with them, or of them, she becomes more and more elevated and refined in her feelings and views. While laboring to cleanse the minds of others from the malaria of moral pollution, her own heart becomes purified, and her soul rises to nearer communion with her God. Such a woman is infinitely better qualified to fulfil the duties of a wife and a mother, than the woman whose *false delicacy* leads her to shun her fallen sister and brother, and shrink from *naming those sins* which she knows exist, but which she is too fastidious to labor by deed and by word to exterminate. Such a woman feels, when she enters upon the marriage relation, that God designed that relation not to debase her to a level with the animal creation, but to increase the happiness and dignity of his creatures. Such a woman comes to the important task of training her children in the nurture and admonition of the Lord, with a soul filled with the greatness of the beings committed to her charge. She sees in her children, creatures bearing the image of God; and she approaches them with reverence, and treats them at all times as moral and accountable beings. Her own mind being purified and elevated, she instils into her children that genuine religion which induces them to keep the commandments of God. Instead of ministering with ceaseless care to their sensual appetites, she teaches them to be temperate in all things. She can converse with her children on any subject relating to their duty to God, can point their attention to those vices which degrade and brutify human nature, without in the least defiling her own mind or theirs. She views herself, and teaches her children to regard themselves as moral beings; and in all their intercourse with their fellow men, to lose the animal nature of man and woman, in the recognition of that immortal mind wherewith Jehovah has blessed and enriched them.

Thine in the bonds of womanhood,

SARAH M. GRIMKE.

LETTER V.

Groton, 8th Mo. 4th, 1837.

MY DEAR SISTER,—I design to devote this letter to a brief examination of the condition of women in Asia and Africa. I believe it will be found that men, in the exercise of their usurped dominion over woman, have almost invariably done one of two things. They have either made slaves of the creatures whom God designed to be their companions and their coadjutors in every moral and intellectual improvement, or they have dressed them like dolls, and used them as toys to amuse their hours of recreation.

I shall commence by stating the degrading practice of **SELLING WOMEN**, which we find prevalent in almost all the Eastern nations.

Among the Jews,—

'Whoever wished for a wife must pay the parents for her, or perform a stipulated period of service; sometimes the parties were solemnly betrothed in childhood, and the price of the bride stipulated.'

In Babylon, they had a yearly custom of a peculiar kind.

'In every district, three men, respectable for their virtue, were chosen to conduct all the marriageable girls to the public assembly. Here they were put up at auction by the public crier, while the magistrate presided over the sales. The most beautiful were sold first, and the rich contended eagerly for a choice. The most ugly, or deformed girl was sold next in succession to the handsomest, and assigned to any person who would take her with the least sum of money. The price given for the beautiful was divided into dowries for the homely.'

Two things may here be noticed; first, the value set upon personal charms, just as a handsome horse commands a high price; and second, the utter disregard which is manifested towards the feelings of woman.

'In no part of the world does the condition of women appear more dreary than in Hindostan. The arbitrary power of a father disposes of them in childhood. When they are married, their husbands have despotic control over them; if unable to support them, they can lend or sell them to a neighbor, and in the Hindoo rage for gambling, wives and children are frequently staked and lost. If they survive their husbands, they must pay implicit obedience to the oldest son; if they have no sons, the nearest male relation holds them in subjection; and if there happen to be no kinsmen, they must be dependent on the chief of the tribe.'

Even the English, who are numerous in Hindostan, have traded in women.

'India has been a great marriage market, on account of the emigration of young enterprising Englishmen, without a corresponding number of women. Some persons actually imported women to the British settlements, in order to sell them to rich Europeans, or nabobs, who would give a good price for them. How the importers acquired a right thus to dispose of them is not mentioned; it is probable that the women themselves, from extreme poverty, or some other cause, consented to become articles of speculation, upon consideration of receiving a certain remuneration. In September, 1818, the following advertisement appeared in the Calcutta Advertiser:

FEMALES RAFFLED FOR.

Be it known, that six fair pretty young ladies, with two sweet engaging children, lately imported from Europe, having the roses of health blooming on their cheeks, and joy sparkling in their eyes, possessing amiable tempers and highly accomplished, whom the most indifferent cannot behold without rapture, are to be raffled for next door to the British gallery.'

The enemy of all good could not have devised a better means of debasing an immortal creature, than by turning her into a saleable commodity; and hence we find that wherever this custom prevails, woman is regarded as a mere machine to answer the purposes of domestic combat or sensual indulgence, or to gratify the taste of her oppressor by a display of personal attractions.

> 'Weighed in the balance with a tyrant's gold,
> Though nature cast her in a heavenly mould.'

I shall now take a brief survey of the EMPLOYMENTS of women in Asia and Africa. In doing this, I have two objects in view; first to show, that women are capable of acquiring as great physical power as men, and secondly to show, that they have been more or less the victims of oppression and contempt.

'The occupations of the ancient Jewish women were laborious. They spent their time in spinning and weaving cloth for garments, and for the covering of the tents, in cooking the food, tending the flocks, grinding the corn, and drawing water from the wells.'

Of Trojan women we know little, but we find that—

'Andromache, though a princess and well beloved by her husband, fed and took care of the horses of Hector.'

So in Persia, women of the middling class see that proper care is taken of the horses. They likewise do all the laborious part of the house work.

'The Hindoo women are engaged in every variety of occupation, according to the caste of their husbands. They cultivate the land, make baskets and mats, bring water in jars, carry manure and various other articles to market in baskets on their heads, cook food, tend children, weave cloth, reel thread and wind cocoons.'

' The Thibetian women of the laboring classes are inured to a great deal of toil. They plant, weed, reap, and thresh grain, and are exposed to the roughest weather, while their indolent husbands are perhaps living at their ease.'

' Females of the lower classes among the Chinese endure as much labor and fatigue as the men. A wife sometimes drags the plough in rice fields with an infant tied upon her back, while her husband performs the less arduous task of holding the plough.'

' The Tartar women in general perform a greater share of labor than the men; for it is a prevalent opinion that they were sent into the world for no other purpose, but to be useful and convenient SLAVES to the stronger sex.' ' Among some of the Tartar tribes of the present day, females manage a horse, hurl a javelin, hunt wild animals, and fight an enemy as well as the men.'

' In the island of Sumatra, the women do all the work, while their husbands lounge in idleness, playing on the flute, with wreaths of globe amaranth on their heads, or racing with each other, without saddle or stirrup, or hunting deer, or gambling away their wives, their children, or themselves. The Battas consider their wives and children as slaves, and sell them whenever they choose.'

' The Moors are indolent to excess. They lie whole days upon their mats, sleeping and smoking, while the women and slaves perform all the labor. Owing to their uncleanly habits, they are much infested with vermin; and as they consider it beneath their dignity to remove this annoyance, the task is imposed on the women. They are very impatient and tyrannical, and for the slightest offence beat their wives most cruelly.'

In looking over the condition of woman as delineated in this letter, how amply do we find the prophecy of Jehovah to Eve fulfilled, ' Thy husband will rule over thee.' And yet we perceive that where the physical strength of woman is called into exercise, there is no inferiority even in this respect; she performs the labor, while man enjoys what are termed the pleasures of life.

I have thought it necessary to adduce various proofs of my assertion, that men have always in some way regarded women as mere instruments of selfish gratification; and hope this sorrowful detail of the wrongs of woman will not be tedious to thee.

Thine in the bonds of womanhood,

SARAH M. GRIMKE.

LETTER VI.

WOMEN IN ASIA AND AFRICA.

Groton, 8th Mo. 15th, 1837.

DEAR FRIEND,—In pursuing the history of woman in different ages and countries, it will be necessary to exhibit her in all the various situations in which she has been placed.

We find her sometimes *filling the throne,* and exercising the functions of royalty. The name of Semiramis is familiar to every reader of ancient history. She succeeded Ninus in the government of the Assyrian empire; and to render her name immortal, built the city of Babylon. Two millions of men were constantly employed upon it. Certain dykes built by order of this queen, to defend the city from inundations, are spoken of as admirable.

Nicotris, wife of Nabonadius, the Evil-Merodach of Scripture, was a woman of great endowments. While her husband indulged in a life of ease and pleasure, she managed the affairs of state with wisdom and prudence.

' Zenobia queen of Palmyra and the East, is the most remarkable among Asiatic women. Her genius struggled with and overcame all the obstacles presented by oriental laws and customs. She knew the Latin, Greek, Syriac, and Egyptian languages; and had drawn up for her own use an abridgement of oriental history. She was the companion and friend of her husband, and accompanied him on his hunting excursions with eagerness and courage equal to his own. She despised the effeminacy of a covered carriage, and often appeared on horseback in military costume. Sometimes she marched several miles on foot, at the head of the troops. Having revenged the murder of her husband, she ascended the throne, and for five years governed Palmyra, Syria, and the East, with wonderful steadiness and wisdom.'

' Previous to the introduction of Mohammedism into Java, women often held the highest offices of government; and when the chief of a district dies, it is even now not uncommon for the widow to retain the authority that belonged to her deceased husband.'

Other instances might be adduced to prove that there is no natural inferiority in woman. Not that I approve of woman's holding the reins of government over man. I maintain that they are equal, and that God never invested fallen man with unlimited power over his fellow man; and I rejoice that circumstances have prevented woman from being more deeply involved in the guilt which appears to be inseparable from political affairs. The few instances which I have mentioned prove that intellect is not sexed; and doubtless if woman had not almost universally been depressed and degraded, the page of history would have exhibited as many eminent statesmen and politicians among women as men. We are much in the situation of the slave. Man has asserted and assumed authority over us. He has, by virtue of his power, deprived us of the advantages of improvement which he has lavishly bestowed upon himself, and then, after having done all he can to take from us the means of proving our equality, and our capability of mental cultivation, he throws upon us the burden of proof that God created man and woman equal, and endowed them, without any reference to sex, with

3

intelligence and responsibilities, as rational and accountable beings. Hence in Hindostan, even women of the higher classes are forbidden to read or write; because the Hindoos think it would inevitably spoil them for domestic life, and assuredly bring some great misfortune upon them. May we not trace to the same feeling, the disadvantages under which women labor even in this country, for want of an education, which would call into exercise the powers of her mind, and fortify her soul with those great moral principles by which she would be qualified to fill *every* department in *social, domestic* and *religious* life with dignity?

In Hindostan, the evidence of women is not received in a court of justice.

In Burmah, their testimony is not deemed equal to that of a man, and they are not allowed to ascend the steps of a court of justice, but are obliged to give their testimony outside of the building.

In Siberia, women are not allowed to step across the foot-prints of men, or reindeer; they are not allowed to eat with men, or to partake of particular dainties. Among many tribes, they seem to be regarded as impure, unholy beings.

'The Mohammedan law forbids pigs, dogs, women and other impure animals to enter a mosque; and the hour of prayers must not be proclaimed by a female, a madman, a drunkard, or a decrepit person.'

Here I am reminded of the resemblance between the situation of women in heathen and Mohammedan countries, and our brethren and sisters of color in this Christian land, where they are despised and cast out as though they were unclean. And on precisely the same ground, because they are said to be inferior.

The treatment of women as wives is almost uniformly the same in all heathen countries.

The ancient Lydians are the only exception that I have met with, and the origin of their peculiar customs is so much obscured by fable, that it is difficult to ascertain the truth. Probably they arose from some great benefit conferred on the state by women.

Among the Druses who reside in the mountains of the Anti Libanus, a wife is often divorced on the slightest pretext. If she ask her husband's permission to go out, and he says,— 'Go,' without adding 'but come back again,' she is divorced.

In Siberia, it is considered a wife's duty to obey the most capricious and unreasonable demands of her husband, without one word of expostulation or inquiry. If her master be dissatisfied with the most trifling particular in her conduct, he tears the cap or veil from her head, and this constitutes a divorce.

A Persian woman, under the dominion of the kindest master, is treated much in the same manner as a favorite animal. To vary her personal graces for his pleasure, is the sole end and aim of her existence. As moral or intellectual beings, it would be better for them to be among the dead than the living. The mother instructs her daughter in all the voluptuous coquetry, by which she herself acquired precarious ascendency over her absolute master; but all that is truly estimable in female character is utterly neglected.

Hence we find women extravagantly fond of

adorning their persons. Regarded as instruments of pleasure, they have been degraded into mere animals, and have found their own gratification principally in the indulgence of personal vanity, because their external charms procured for them, at least a temporary ascendency over those, who held in their hands the reins of government. A few instances must suffice, or I shall exceed the limits I have prescribed to myself in this letter.

During the magnificent prosperity of Israel, marriages were conducted with great pomp; and with the progress of luxury and refinement, women became expensive, rather than profitable in a pecuniary point of view. Hence probably arose the custom of wealthy parents giving a handsome dowry with their daughters. On the day of the nuptials, the bride was conducted by her female relations to the bath, where she was anointed with the choicest perfumes, her hair perfumed and braided, her eyebrows deepened with black powder, and the tips of her fingers tinged with rose color. She was then arrayed in a marriage robe of brilliant color; the girdle and bracelets were more or less costly.

Notwithstanding the Chinese women have no opportunity to rival each other in the conquest of hearts, they are nevertheless very fond of ornaments. Bunches of silver or gilt flowers are always interspersed among their ringlets, and someties they wear the Chinese phœnix made of silver gilt. It moves with the slightest motion of the wearer, and the spreading tail forms a glittering aigrette on the middle of the head, and the wings wave over the front. Yet a Chinese ballad says,—The pearls and precious stones, the silk and gold with which a coquette so studiously bedecks herself, are a transparent varnish which makes all her defects the more apparent.

The Moorish women have generally a great passion for ornament. They decorate their persons with heavy gold ear-rings, necklaces of amber, coral and gold; gold bracelets; gold chains and silver bells for the ankles; rings on the fingers, &c. &c. The poorer class wear glass beads around the head, and curl the hair in large ringlets. Men are proud of having their wives handsomely dressed.

The Moors are not peculiar in this fancy. Christian men still admire women who adorn their persons to gratify the lust of the eye and the pride of life. Women, says a Brahminical expositor, are characterized by an inordinate love of jewels, fine clothes, &c. &c. I cannot deny this charge, but it is only one among many instances, wherein men have reproached us with those very faults and vices which their own treatment has engendered. Is it any matter of surprise that women, when unnaturally deprived of the means of cultivating their minds, of objects which would elevate and refine their passions and affections, should seek gratification in the toys and the trifles which now too generally engage their attention?

I cannot close this, without acknowledging the assistance and information I have derived, and shall continue to derive on this part of my subject, from a valuable work entitled 'Condition of' Women, by Lydia M Child.' It is worth the perusal of every one who is interested in the subject.

Thine in the bonds of womanhood,
SARAH M. GRIMKE.

LETTER VII.

CONDITION IN SOME PARTS OF EUROPE AND
AMERICA.

Brookline, 8th Mo., 22d, 1837.

DEAR SISTER,—I now come to the consideration of the condition of woman in Europe.—
In this portion of the world, she does not appear to have been as uniformly or as deeply debased, as in Eastern countries; yet we shall find little in her history which can yield us satisfaction, when we regard the high station she was designed to occupy as a *moral and intellectual* being.

In Greece, if we may judge from what Eustathius says, 'women should keep within doors, and there talk,'—we may conclude, that in general their occupations were chiefly domestic. Thucydides also declares, that 'she was the best woman, of whom the least was said, either of good or of harm.' The heathen philosophers doubtless wished to keep woman in her '*appropriate sphere ;*' and we find our clerical brethren of the present day re-echoing these pagan sentiments, and endeavoring to drive woman from the field of moral labor and intellectual culture, to occupy her talents in the pursuit

of those employments which will enable her to
regale the palate of her lord with the delica-
cies of the table, and in every possible way
minister to his animal comfort and gratification.
In my humble opinion, woman has long enough
subserved the interests of man; and in the
spirit of self-sacrifice, submitted almost without
remonstrance to his oppression; and now that
her attention is solicited to the subject of her
rights, her privileges and her duties, I would
entreat her to double her diligence in the performance of all her obligations as a *wife*, a *mother*, a *sister*, and a *daughter*. Let us remem-
ber that our claim to stand on perfect equality
with our brethren, can only be substantiated by
a scrupulous attention to our domestic duties, as
well as by aiding in the great work of moral
reformation—a work which is now calling for
the energies and consecrated powers of every
man and woman who desires to see the Redeemer's kingdom established on earth. That
man must indeed be narrow minded, and can
have but a poor conception of the power of
moral truth on the female heart, who supposes
that a correct view of her own rights can make
woman *less solicitous to fill up every department
of duty.* If it should have this effect, it must
be because she has not taken a comprehensive
view of the whole snbject.

In the history of Rome, we find a little spot
of sunshine in the valley where woman has
been destined to live, unable from her lowly situation to take an expansive view of that field
of moral and mental improvement, which she
should have been busy in cultivating.

'In the earliest and best days of Rome, the first magistrates and generals of armies ploughed their own fields, and

threshed their own grain. Integrity, industry and simplicity, were the prevailing virtues of the times; and the character of woman was, as it always must be, graduated in a
degree by that of man. Columella says, Roman husbands,
having completed the labors of the day, entered their houses
free from all care, and there enjoyed perfect repose. There
reigned union and concord and industry, supported by mu-
tual affections. The most beautiful woman depended for
distinction on her economy and endeavors to assist in crown-
ing her husband's diligence with prosperity. All was in
common between them; nothing was thought to belong more
to one than another. The wife by her assiduity and activity within doors, equalled and seconded the industry and la
bor of her husband.'

In the then state of the world, we may conclude from this description, that woman enjoyed as much happiness as was consistent with
that comparatively unimproved condition of our
species; but now a new and vast sphere of usefulness is opened to her, and she is pressed by
surrounding circumstances to come up to the
help of the Lord against the giant sins which
desolate our beloved country. Shall woman
shrink from duty in this exigency, and retiring
within her own domestic circle, delight herself in the abundance of her own selfish enjoyments. Shall she rejoice in her home, her husband, her children, and forget her brethren and
sisters in bondage, who know not what it is to
call a spot of earth their own, whose husbands and wives are torn from them by relent-
less tyrants, and whose children are snatch-
ed from their arms by their unfeeling task-mas-
ters, whenever interest, or convenience, tempts
them to this sacrilegious act? Shall woman
disregard the situation of thousands of her fellow creatures, who are the victims of intemperance and licentiousness, and retreating to
the privacy of her own comfortable home, be
satisfied that her whole duty is performed, when

she can exhibit ' her children well clad and smiling, and her table neatly spread with wholesome provisions?' Shall she, because ' her house is her *home*,' refuse her aid and her sympathy to the down trodden slave, to the poor unhappy outcasts who are deprived of those blessings which she so highly prizes? Did God give her those blessings to steel her heart to the sufferings of her fellow creatures? Did he grant her the possession of husband and children, to dry up the fountains of feeling for those who know not the consolations of tenderness and reciprocal affection? Ah no! for every such blessing, God demands a grateful heart; and woman must be recreant to her duty, if she can quietly sit down in the enjoyments of her own domestic circle, and not exert herself to procure the same happiness for others.

But it is said woman has a mighty weapon in secret prayer. She has, I acknowledge, *in common with man;* but the woman who prays in sincerity for the regeneration of this guilty world, will accompany her prayers by her labors. A friend of mine remarked—' I was sitting in my chamber, weeping over the miseries of the slave, and putting up my petitions for his deliverance from bondage; when in the midst of my meditations, it occurred to me that my tears, unaided by effort, could never melt the chain of the slave. I must be up and doing.' She is now an active abolitionist—her prayers and her works go hand in hand.

I am here reminded of what a slave once said to his master, a Methodist minister. The slaveholder inquired, 'How did you like my sermon to-day?' 'Very good, master, but it did not preach me free.'

Oh, my sisters, suffer me to entreat you to assert your privileges, and to perform your duties as moral beings. Be not dismayed at the ridicule of man; it is a weapon worthy only of little minds, and is employed by those who feel that they cannot convince our judgment. Be not alarmed at contumely, or scorn; we must expect this. I pray that we may meet it with forbearance and love; and that nothing may drive us from the performance of our high and holy duties. Let us 'cease from man, whose breath is in his nostrils, for wherein is he to be accounted of?' and press forward in all the great moral enterprises of the age, leaning *only* on the arm of our Beloved.

But I must return to the subject I commenced with, viz. the condition of woman in Europe.

'The northern nations bore a general resemblance to each other. War and hunting were considered the only honorable occupations for men, and all other employments were left to women and slaves. Even the Visigoths, on the coasts of Spain, left their fields and flocks to the care of women. The people who inhabit the vast extent of country between the Black sea and the North sea, are divided into various distinct races. The women are generally very industrious; even in their walks, they carry a portable distaff, and spin every step of the way. Both Croatian and Walachian women perform all the agricultural operations in addition to their own domestic concerns.'

Speaking of the Morlachian women, M. Fortis says, Being treated like beasts of burden, and expected to endure submissively every species of hardship, they naturally become very dirty and careless in their habits.'

The Cossack women afford a contrast to this disgusting picture. They are very cleanly and industrious, and in the absence of their husbands, supply their places by taking charge of all their usual occupations, in addition to their own. It is rare for a Cossack woman not to know some trade, such as dyeing cloth, tanning leather, &c.

The condition of Polish and Russian serfs in modern times is about the same. The Polish women have scarcely clothing enough for decency, and they are subjected to great hardships and privations. 'In Russia, women have been seen paving the streets, and performing other similar drudgery. In Finland, they work like beasts of burden, and may be seen for hours in snow water, up to the middle, tugging at boats and sledges.'

In Flanders and in France, women are engaged in performing laborious tasks; and even in England, it is not unusual to see them scraping up manure from the streets with their hands, and gathering it into baskets.

In Greece, even now the women plough and carry heavy burdens, while the lordly master of the family may be seen walking before them without any incumbrance.*

---

* Since the preceding letters were in type, I have met with the following account in a French work entitled ' De l' education des meres de famille on de la civilization du Genre Humain par les femmes,' printed at Brussels in 1837. ' The periodicals have lately published the following circumstance from the journal of an English physician, who travelled in the East. He visited a slave market, where he saw about twenty Greek women half naked, lying on the ground waiting for a purchaser. One of them attracted the attention of an old Turk. The barbarian examined her shoulders, her legs, her ears, her mouth, her neck, with the minutest care, just as a horse is examined, and during the inspection, the merchant praised the beauty of her eyes. the ele-

Generally speaking, however, there is much more comparative equality of labor between the sexes in Europe than among the Orientals.

I shall close this letter with a brief survey of the condition of women among the Aborigines of America.

'Before America was settled by Europeans, it was inhabited by Indian tribes, which greatly resembled each other in the treatment of their women. Every thing, except war and hunting, was considered beneath the dignity of man.— During long and wearisome marches, women were obliged to carry children, provisions and hammocks on their shoulders; they had the sole care of the horses and dogs, cut wood, pitched the tents, raised the corn, and made the clothing. When the husband killed game, he left it by a tree in the forest, returned home, and sent his wife several miles in search of it. In most of the tribes, women were not allowed to eat and drink with men, but stood and served them, and then ate what they left.'

The following affecting anecdote may give some idea of the sufferings of these women:

'Father Joseph reproved a female savage for destroying her infant daughter. She replied, "I wish my mother had thus prevented the manifold sufferings I have endured. Consider, father, our deplorable situation. Our husbands go out to hunt; we are dragged along with one infant at our breast, and another in a basket. Though tired with long walking, we are not allowed to sleep when we return, but must labor all night in grinding maize and making chica for them.— They get drunk and beat us, draw us by the hair of the head, and tread us under foot. Would to God my mother had put me under ground the moment I was born." '

gance of her shape, and other perfections; he protested that the poor girl was but thirteen years of age, &c. After a severe scrutiny and some dispute about the price, she was sold body and soul for 1375 francs. The soul, it is true, was accounted of little value in the bargain. The unfortunate creature, half fainting in the arms of her mother, implored help in the most touching accents, but it availed nothing— This infernal scene passed in Europe in 1829, only 600 leagues from Paris and Loudon, the two capitals of the human species, and at the time in which I write, it is the living history of two thirds of the inhabitants of the earth.'

In Greenland, the situation of woman is equally deplorable. The men hunt bears and catch seals; but when they have towed their booty to land, they would consider it a disgrace to help the women drag it home, or skin and dress it. They often stand and look idly on, while their wives are staggering beneath the load that almost bends them to the earth. The women are cooks, butchers, masons, curriers, shoemakers and tailors. They will manage a boat in the roughest seas, and will often push off from the shore in the midst of a storm, that would make the hardiest European sailor tremble.

The page of history teems with woman's wrongs, and it is wet with woman's tears.— For the sake of my degraded sex every where, and for the sake of my brethren, who suffer just in proportion as they place woman lower in the scale of creation than man; lower than her Creator placed her, I entreat my sisters to arise in all the majesty of moral power, in all the dignity of immortal beings, and plant themselves, side by side, on the platform of human rights, with man, to whom they were designed to be companions, equals and helpers in every good word and work.

Thine in the bonds of womanhood,

SARAH M. GRIMKE.

LETTER VIII.

ON THE CONDITION OF WOMEN IN THE UNITED
STATES.

Brookline, 1837.

MY DEAR SISTER,—I have now taken a brief
survey of the condition of woman in various
parts of the world. I regret that my time has
been so much occupied by other things, that I
have been unable to bestow that attention upon
the subject which it merits, and that my constant change of place has prevented me from
having access to books, which might probably
have assisted me in this part of my work. I
hope that the principles I have asserted will
claim the attention of some of my sex, who
may be able to bring into view, more thoroughly than I have done, the situation and degradation of woman. I shall now proceed to make
a few remarks on the condition of women in
my own country.

During the early part of my life, my lot was
cast among the butterflies of the *fashionable*
world; and of this class of women, I am constrained to say, both from experience and observation, that their education is miserably defi-
cient; that they are taught to regard marriage
as the one thing needful, the only avenue to

distinction; hence to attract the notice and win the attentions of men, by their external charms, is the chief business of fashionable girls. They seldom think that men will be allured by intellectual acquirements, because they find, that where any mental superiority exists, a woman is generally shunned and regarded as stepping out of her 'appropriate sphere,' which, in their view, is to dress, to dance, to set out to the best possible advantage her person, to read the novels which inundate the press, and which do more to destroy her character as a rational creature, than any thing else. Fashionable women regard themselves, and are regarded by men, as pretty toys or as mere instruments of pleasure; and the vacuity of mind, the heartlessness, the frivolity which is the necessary result of this false and debasing estimate of women, can only be fully understood by those who have mingled in the folly and wickedness of fashionable life; and who have been called from such pursuits by the voice of the Lord Jesus, inviting their weary and heavy laden souls to come unto Him and learn of Him, that they may find something worthy of their immortal spirit, and their intellectual powers; that they may learn the high and holy purposes of their creation, and consecrate themselves unto the service of God; and not, as is now the case, to the pleasure of man.

There is another and much more numerous class in this country, who are withdrawn by education or circumstances from the circle of fashionable amusements, but who are brought up with the dangerous and absurd idea, that *marriage* is a kind of preferment; and that to be able to keep their husband's house, and render his situation comfortable, is the end of her being. Much that she does and says and thinks is done in reference to this situation; and to be married is too often held up to the view of girls as the sine qua non of human happiness and human existence. For this purpose more than for any other,I verily believe the majority of girls are trained. This is demonstrated bythe imperfect education which is bestowed upon them,and the little pains taken to cultivate their minds, after they leave school, by the little time allowed them for reading, and by the idea being constantly inculcated, that although all household concerns should be attended to with scrupulous punctuality at particular seasons, the improvement of their intellectual capacities is only a secondary consideration, and may serve as an occupation to fill up the odds and ends of time. In most families, it is considered a matter of far more consequence to call a girl off from making a pie, or a pudding, than to interrupt her whilst engaged in her studies. This mode of training necessarily exalts, in their view, the animal above the intellectual and spiritual nature, and teaches women to regard themselves as a kind of machinery, necessary to keep the domestic engine in order, but of little value as the *intelligent* companions of men.

Let no one think, from these remarks, that I regard a knowledge of housewifery as beneath the acquisition of women. Far from it: I believe that a complete knowledge of household affairs is an indispensable requisite in a woman's education,—that by the mistress of a family, whether married or single, doing her duty thoroughly and *understandingly*, the happiness of the family is increased to an incalculable degree, os well as a vast amount of time and money saved. All I complain of is, that our education consists so almost exclusively in culinary and other manual operations. I do long to see the time, when it will no longer be necessary for women to expend so many precious hours in furnishing 'a well spread table,' but that their husbands will forego some of their accustomed indulgences in this way, and encourage their wives to devote some portion of their time to mental cultivation, even at the expense of having to dine sometimes on baked potatoes, or bread and butter.

I believe the sentiment expressed by the author of 'Live and let Live,' is true:

'Other things being equal, a woman of the highest mental endowments will always be the best housekeeper, for domestic economy, is a science that brings into action the qualities of the mind, as well as the graces of the heart. A quick perception, judgment, discrimination, decision and order are high attributes of mind, and are all in daily exercise in the well ordering of a family. If a sensible woman, an intellectual woman, a woman of genius, is not a good housewife, it is not because she is either, or all of those, but because there is some deficiency in her character, or some omission of duty which should make her very humble, instead of her indulging in any secret self-complacency on account of a certain superiority, which only aggravates her fault.'

The influence of women over the minds and character of *children* of both sexes, is allowed to be far greater than that of men. This being the case by the very ordering of nature, women should be prepared by education for the performance of their sacred duties as mothers and as sisters. A late American writer,* speaking on this subject, says in reference to an article in the Westminster Review:

* Thomas S. Grimke.

4

' I agree entirely with the writer in the high estimate which he places on female education, and have long since been satisfied, that the subject not only merits, but *imperiously demands* a thorough reconsideration. The whole scheme must, in my opinion, be reconstructed. The great elements of usefulness and duty are too little attended to. Women ought, in my view of the subject, to approach to the best education now given to men, (I except mathematics and the classics,) far more I believe than has ever yet been attempted. Give me a host of educated, pious mothers and sisters, and I will do more to revolutionize a country, in moral and religious taste, in manners and in social virtues and intellectual cultivation, than I can possibly do in double or treble the time, with a similar host of educated men. I cannot but think that the miserable condition of the great body of the people in all ancient communities, is to be ascribed in a very great degree to the degradation of women.'

There is another way in which the general opinion, that women are inferior to men, is manifested, that bears with tremendous effect on the laboring class, and indeed on almost all who are obliged to earn a subsistence, whether it be by mental or physical exertion—I allude to the disproportionate value set on the time and labor of men and of women. A man who is engaged in teaching, can always, I believe, command a higher price for tuition than a woman—even when he teaches the same branches, and is not in any respect superior to the woman. This I know is the case in boarding and other schools with which I have been acquainted, and it is so in every occupation in which the sexes engage indiscriminately. As for example, in tailoring, a man has twice, or three times as much for making a waistcoat or pantaloons as a woman, although the work done by each may be equally good. In those employments which are peculiar to women, their time is estimated at only half the value of that of men. A woman who goes out to wash, works as hard in proportion as a wood sawyer, or a coal heaver, but she is not generally able to make more than half as much by a day's work. The low remuneration which women receive for their work, has claimed the attention of a few philanthropists, and I hope it will continue to do so until some remedy is applied for this enormous evil. I have known a widow, left with four or five children, to provide for, unable to leave home because her helpless babes demand her attention, compelled to earn a scanty subsistence, by making coarse shirts at 12 1-2 cents a piece, or by taking in washing, for which she was paid by some wealthy persons 12 1-2 cents per dozen. All these things evince the low estimation in which woman is held. There is yet another and more disastrous consequence arising from this unscriptural notion—women being educated, from earliest childhood, to regard themselves as inferior creatures, have not that self-respect which conscious equality would engender, and hence when their virtue is assailed, they yield to temptation with facility, under the idea that it rather exalts than debases them, to be connected with a superior being.

There is another class of women in this country, to whom I cannot refer, without feelings of the deepest shame and sorrow. I allude to our female slaves. Our southern cities are whelmed beneath a tide of pollution; the virtue of female slaves is wholly at the mercy of irresponsible tyrants, and women are bought and sold in our slave markets, to gratify the brutal lust of those who bear the name of Christians. In our slave States, if amid all her degradation and ignorance, a woman desires to preserve her virtue unsullied, she is either bribed or whipped into compliance, or if she dares resist her seducer,

her life by the laws of some of the slave States
may be, and has actually been sacrificed to the
fury of disappointed passion. Where such
laws do not exist, the power which is necessarily vested in the master over his property, leaves
the defenceless slave entirely at his mercy, and
the sufferings of some females on this account,
both physical and mental, are intense. Mr.
Gholson, in the House of Delegates of Virginia,
in 1832, said, ' He really had been under the
impression that he owned his slaves. He had
lately purchased four women and ten children,
in whom he thought he had obtained a great
bargain ; for he supposed they were his own
property, *as were his brood mares.*' But even
if any laws existed in the United States, as in
Athens formerly, for the protection of female
slaves, they would be null and void, because the
evidence of a colored person is not admitted
against a white, in any of our Courts of Justice
in the slave States. ' In Athens, if a female
slave had cause to complain of any want of respect to the laws of modesty, she could seek
the protection of the temple, and demand a
change of owners ; and such appeals were never discountenanced, or neglected by the magistrate.' In Christian America, the slave has no
refuge from unbridled cruelty and lust.

S. A. Forrall, speaking of the state of morals
at the South, says, ' Negresses when young and
likely, are often employed by the planter, or his
friends, to administer to their sensual desires.
This frequently is a matter of speculation, for
if the offspring, a mulatto, be a handsome female, 800 or 1000 dollars may be obtained for
her in the New Orleans market. It is an oc-
currence of no uncommon nature to see a Chris-

tian father sell his own daughter, and the brother his own sister.' The following is copied by
the N. Y. Evening Star from the Picayune, a
paper published in New Orleans. 'A very
beautiful girl, belonging to the estate of John
French, a deceased gambler at New Orleans,
was sold a few days since for the round sum of
$7,000. An ugly-looking bachelor named
Gouch, a member of the Council of one of the
Principalities, was the purchaser. The girl is
a brunette; remarkable for her beauty and intelligence, and there was considerable contention, who should be the purchaser. She was,
however, persuaded to accept Gouch, he having
made her princely promises.' I will add but
one more from the numerous testimonies respecting the degradation of female slaves, and
the licentiousness of the South. It is from the
Circular of the Kentucky Union, for the moral
and religious improvement of the colored race.
' To the female character among our black pop-
ulation, we cannot allude but with feelings of
the bitterest shame. A similar condition of
moral pollution and utter disregard of a pure
and virtuous reputation, is to be found *only
without the pale of Christendom.* That such
a state of society should exist in a Christian
nation, claiming to be the most enlightened
upon earth, without calling forth any *particular
attention* to its existence, though ever before
our eyes and *in our* families, is a moral phe-
nomenon at once unaccountable and disgraceful.' Nor does the colored woman suffer alone :
the moral purity of the white woman is deeply
contaminated. In the daily habit of seeing the
virtue of her enslaved sister sacrificed without
hesitancy or remorse, she looks upon the crimes

of seduction and illicit intercourse without hor-
ror, and although not personally involved in the
guilt, she loses that value for innocence in her
own, as well as the other sex, which is one of
the strongest safeguards to virtue. She lives
in habitual intercourse with men, whom she
knows to be polluted by licentiousness, and often
is she compelled to witness in her own domestic circle, those disgusting and heart-sickening
jealousies and strifes which disgraced and dis-
tracted the family of Abraham. In addition to
all this, the female slaves suffer every species
of degradation and cruelty, which the most
wanton barbarity can inflict; they are indecent-
ly divested of their clothing, sometimes tied up
and severely whipped, sometimes prostrated on
the earth, while their naked bodies are torn by
the scorpion lash.

> ‘ The whip on WOMAN’S shrinking flesh !
> Our soil yet reddening with the stains
> Caught from her scourging warm and fresh.’

Can any American woman look at these scenes
of shocking licentiousness and cruelty, and fold
her hands in apathy ,and say, ‘ I have nothing to
do with slavery ’ ? *She cannot and be guiltless.*

I cannot close this letter, without saying a
few words on the benefits to be derived by men,
as well as women, from the opinions I advocate
relative to the equality of the sexes. Many
women are now supported, in idleness and extravagance, by the industry of their husbands,
fathers, or brothers, who are compelled to toil
out their existence, at the counting house, or in
the printing office, or some other laborious occupation, while the wife and daughters and sisters take no part in the support of the family,
and appear to think that their sole business is

to spend the hard bought earnings of their male friends. I deeply regret such a state of things, because I believe that if women felt their responsibility, for the support of themselves, or their families it would add strength and dignity to their characters, and teach them more true sympathy for their husbands, than is now generally manifested,—a sympathy which would be exhibited by actions as well as words. Our brethren may reject my doctrine, because it runs counter to common opinions, and because it wounds their pride; but I believe they would be 'partakers of the benefit' resulting from the Equality of the Sexes, and would find that woman, as their equal, was unspeakably more valuable than woman as their inferior, both as a moral and an intellectual being.

Thine in the bonds of womanhood,

SARAH M. GRIMKE.

LETTER IX

Brookline, 8th Mo. 25th, 1837.

MY DEAR SISTER,—It seems necessary to glance at the conduct of women under circumstances which place them in juxtaposition with men, although I regard it as entirely unimportant in proving the moral equality of the sexes; because I condemn, in both. the exercise of that brute force which is as contrary to the law of God in men as in women; still, as a part of our history, I shall notice some instances of courage exhibited by females

'Philippa, wife of Edward III., was the principal cause of the victory gained over the Scots at Neville Cross. In the absence of her husband, she rode among the troops, and exhorted them to "be of good courage."' Jane, Countess of Mountfort, and a contemporary of Philippa, likewise possessed a great share of physical courage. The history of Joan of Arc is too familiar to need repetition. During the reign of James II. a singular instance of female intrepidity occurred in Scotland. Sir John Cochrane being condemned to be hung, his daughter twice disguised herself, and robbed the mail that brought his death warrant. In he mean time, his pardon was obtained from the King. Instances might be multiplied, but it is unnecessary. I shall therefore close these proofs of female courage with one more fact. ' During the revolutionary war, the women shared in the patriotism and bravery of the men. Several individuals carried their enthusiasm so far as to enter the army, where they faced all the perils and fatigues of the camp, until the close of the war.

When I view my countrywomen in the character of soldiers, or even behold them loading fire arms and moulding bullets for their brethren to destroy men's lives, I cannot refrain a sigh. I cannot but contrast their conduct at that solemn crisis with the conduct of those women who followed their Lord and Master with unresisting submission, to Calvary's Mount. With the precepts and example of a crucified Redeemer, who, in that sublime precept, ' Resist not evil,' has interdicted to his disciples all war and all violence, and taught us that the spirit of retaliation for injuries, whether in the camp, or at the fire-side, is wholly at variance with the peaceful religion he came to promulgate. How little do we comprehend that simple truth, ' By this shall all men know that ye are my disciples, if ye have *love one to another.*'

Women have sometimes distinguished themselves in a way more consistent with their duties as moral beings. During the war between the Romans and the Sabines, the Sabine women who had been carried off by the Romans, repaired to the Sabine camp, dressed in deep mourning, with their little ones in their arms, to soften, if possible, the feelings of their parents. They knelt at the feet of their relatives ; and when Hersilia, the wife of Romulus, described the kindness of their husbands, and their unwillingness to be separated from them, their fathers yielded to their entreaties, and an alliance was soon agreed upon. In consequence of this important service, peculiar privileges were conferred on women by the Romans. Brutus said of his wife, 'I must not answer Portia in the words of Hector, "Mind your wheel, and to your maids give law," for in courage, activity and concern for her country's freedom, she is inferior to none of us.' After the fatal battle of Cannæ, the Roman women consecrated all their ornaments to the service of the state. But when the triumvirs attempted to tax them for the expenses of carrying on a civil war, they resisted the innovation. They chose Hortensia for their speaker, and went in a body to the market-place to expostulate with the magistrates. The triumvirs wished to drive them away, but they were compelled to yield to the wishes of the people, and give the women a hearing. Hortensia pleaded so well the cause of her sisters, who resolved that they would not voluntarily aid in a *civil war*, that the number of women taxed was reduced from 1400 to 400.

In the wars of the Guelphs and the Ghibbelines, the emperor Conrad refused all terms of capitulation to the garrison of Winnisberg, but he granted the request of the women to pass out in safety with such of their effects as they could carry themselves. Accordingly, they issued from the besieged city, each bearing on her shoulders a husband, son, father, or brother. They passed unmolested through the enemy's camp, which rung with acclamations of applause.

During our struggle for independence, the women were as exemplary as the men in various instances of self-denial : they refused every article of decoration for their persons; foreign elegances were laid aside, and they cheerfully abstained from luxuries for their tables.

English history presents many instances of women exercising prerogatives now denied them. In an action at law, it has been determined that an unmarried woman, having a freehold, might vote for members of Parliament; and it is recorded that lady Packington returned two. Lady Broughton was keeper of the gatehouse prison. And in a much later period, a woman was appointed governor of the house of correction at Chelmsford, by order of the court. In the reign of George II. the minister of Clerkenwell was chosen by a majority of women. The office of grand chamberlain in 1822 was filled by two women; and that of clerk of the crown, in the court of king's bench, has been granted to a female. The celebrated Anne, countess of Pembroke, held the hereditary office of sheriff of Westmoreland, and exercised it in person, sitting on the bench with the judges.

I need hardly advert to the names of Elizabeth of England, Maria Theresa of Germany, Catharine of Russia, and Isabella of Spain, to prove that women are capable of swaying the sceptre of royalty. The page of history proves incontestibly, not only that they are as well qualified to do so as men, but that there has been a comparatively greater proportion of good queens, than of good kings; women who have purchased their celebrity by individual strength of character.

I mention these women only to prove that intellect is not sexed; that strength of mind is not sexed; and that our views about the duties of men and the duties of women, the sphere of man and the sphere of woman, are mere arbitrary opinions, differing in different ages and countries, and dependant solely on the will and judgment of erring mortals.

As moral and responsible beings, men and women have the same sphere of action, and the same duties devolve upon both ; but no one can doubt that the duties of each vary according to circumstances; that a father and a mother, a husband and a wife, have sacred obligations resting on them, which cannot possibly belong to those who do not sustain these relations. But these duties and responsibilities do not attach to them as men and as women, but as parents, husbands, and wives.

Thine in the bonds of womanhood,

SARAH M. GRIMKE.

LETTER X.

Brookline, 8th Mo. 1837.

MY DEAR SISTER,—It will scarcely be denied, I presume, that, as a general rule, men do not desire the improvement of women. There are few instances of men who are magnanimous enough to be entirely willing that women should know more than themselves, on any subjects except dress and cookery; and, indeed, this necessarily flows from their assumption of superiority. As *they* have determined that Jehovah has placed woman on a lower platform than man, they of course wish to keep her there; and hence the noble faculties of our minds are crushed, and our reasoning powers are almost wholly uncultivated.

A writer in the time of Charles I. says—' She that knoweth how to compound a pudding, is more 'desirable than she who skilfully compounded a poem. A female poet I mislike at all times.' Within the last century, it has been gravely asserted that, ' chemistry enough to keep the pot boiling, and geography enough to know the location of the different rooms in her house, is learning sufficient for a woman.' Byron, who was too sensual to conceive of a pure and perfect companionship between the sexes, would limit a woman's library to a Bible and cookery book. I have myself heard men, who knew for themselves the value of intellectual culture, say they cared very little for a wife who could not make a pudding, and smile with contempt at the ardent thirst for knowledge exhibited by some women.

But all this is miserable wit and worse philosophy. It exhibits that passion for the gratification of a pampered appetite, which is beneath those who claim to be so far above us, and may justly be placed on a par with the policy of the slaveholder, who says that men will be better slaves, if they are not permitted to learn to read.

In spite, however, of the obstacles which impede the progress of women towards that state of high mental cultivation for which her Creator prepared her, the tendency towards the universal dissemination of knowledge has had its influence on their destinies ; and in all ages, a few have surmounted every hindrance, and proved, beyond dispute, that they have talents equal to their brethren.

Cornelia, the daughter of Scipio Africanus, was distinguished for virtue, learning and good sense. She wrote and spoke with uncommon elegance and purity. Cicero and Quinctilian bestow high praise upon her letters, and the eloquence of her children was attributed to her careful superintendence. This reminds me of a remark made by my brother, Thomas S. Grimke, when speaking of the importance of women being well educated, that ' educated men would never make educated women, but educated women would make educated men.'

I believe the sentiment is correct, because if the wealth of latent intellect among women was fully evolved and improved, they would rejoice to communicate to their sons all their own knowledge, and inspire them with desires to drink from the fountain of literature.

I pass over many interesting proofs of the intellectual powers of women; but I must not omit glancing at the age of chivalry, which has been compared to a golden thread running through the dark ages. During this remarkable era, women who, before this period, had been subject to every species of oppression and neglect, were suddenly elevated into deities, and worshipped with a mad fanaticism. It is not improbable, however, that even the absurdities of chivalry were beneficial to women, as it raised them from that extreme degradation to which they had been condemned, and prepared the way for them to be permitted to enjoy some scattered rays from the sun of science and literature. As the age of knight-errantry declined, men began to take pride in learning, and women shared the advantages which this change produced. Women preached in public, supported controversies, published and defended theses, filled the chairs of philosophy and law, harangued the popes in Latin, wrote Greek and read Hebrew. Nuns wrote poetry, women of rank became divines, and young girls publicly exhorted Christian princes to take up arms for the recovery of the holy sepulchre. Hypatia, daughter of Theon of Alexandria, succeeded her father in the government of the Platonic school, and filled with reputation a seat, where many celebrated philosophers had taught. The people regarded her as an oracle, and magis trates consulted her in all important cases. No reproach was ever uttered against the perfect purity of her manners. She was unembarrassed in large assemblies of men, because their admiration was tempered with the most scrupulous respect. In the 13th century, a young lady of Bologna pronounced a Latin oration at the age of twenty-three. At twenty-six, she took the degree of doctor of laws, and began publicly to expound Justinian. At thirty, she was elevated to a professor's chair, and taught the law to a crowd of scholars from all nations. Italy produced many learned and gifted women, among whom, perhaps none was more celebrated than Victoria Colonna, Marchioness of Pescara. In Spain, Isabella of Rosera converted Jews by her eloquent preaching;' and in England the names of many women, from Lady Jane Gray down to Harriet Martineau, are familiar to every reader of history. Of the last mentioned authoress, Lord Brougham said that her writings on political economy were doing more good than those of any man in England. There is a contemporary of Harriet Martineau, who has recently rendered valuable services to her country. She presented a memorial to Parliament, stating the dangerous parts of the coast, where light-houses were needed, and at her suggestion, several were erected. She keeps a life-boat and sailors in her pay, and has been the means of saving many lives. Although she has been deprived of the use of her limbs since early childhood, yet even when the storm is unusually severe, she goes herself on the beach in her carriage, that she may be sure her men perform their duty. She understands several languages, and is now engaged in writing a work on the Northern languages of Europe. 'In Germany, the influence of women on literature is considerable, though less obvious than in some other countries. Literary families frequently meet at each others houses, and learned and intelligent women are often the brightest ornaments of these social circles.' France has produced many distinguished women, whose names are familiar to every lover of literature. And I believe it is conceded universally, that Madame de Stael was intellectually the greatest woman that ever lived. The United States have produced several female writers, some of whom have talents of the highest order. But women, even in this free republic, do not enjoy *all* the intellectual advantages of men, although there is a perceptible improvement within the last ten or twenty years; and I trust there is a desire awakened in my sisters for solid acquirements, which will elevate them to their 'appropriate sphere,' and enable them to 'adorn the doctrine of God our Saviour in all things.'

Thine in the bonds of womanhood,

SARAH M. GRIMKE.

5

LETTER XI.

Brookline, 9th Mo., 1837.

My Dear Sister,—When I view woman as
an immortal being, travelling through this world
to that city whose builder and maker is God,—
when I contemplate her in all the sublimity of
her spiritual existence, bearing the image and
superscription of Jehovah, emanating from Him
and partaking of his nature, and destined, if
she fulfils her duty, to dwell with him through
the endless ages of eternity,—I mourn that she
has lived so far below her privileges and her
obligations, as a rational and accountable creature; and I ardently long to behold her occupy-
ing that sphere in which I believe her Creator
designed her to move.

Woman, in all ages and countries, has been
the scoff and the jest of her lordly master. If
she attempted, like him, to improve her mind,
she was ridiculed as pedantic, and driven from
the temple of science and literature by coarse
attacks and vulgar sarcasms. If she yielded to
the pressure of circumstances, and sought relief
from the monotony of existence by resorting to
the theatre and the ball-room, by ornamenting
her person with flowers and with jewels, while

her mind was empty and her heart desolate; she was still the mark at which wit and satire and cruelty levelled their arrows.

'Woman,' says Adam Clarke, 'has been invidiously defined, *an animal of dress.* How long will they permit themselves to be thus degraded?' I have been an attentive observer of my sex, and I am constrained to believe that the passion for dress, which so generally characterizes them, is one cause why there so is little of that solid improvement and weight of character which might be acquired under almost any circumstances, if the mind were not occupied by the love of admiration, and the desire to gratify personal vanity. I have already adduced some instances to prove the inordinate love of dress, which is exhibited by women in a state of heathenism; I shall, therefore, confine myself now to what are called Christian countres; only remarking that previous to the introauction of Christianity into the Roman empire, the extravagance of apparel had arisen to an unprecedented height. 'Jewels, expensive embroidery, and delicious perfumes, were used in great profusion by those who could afford them.' The holy religion of Jesus Christ came in at this period, and stript luxury and wealth of all their false attractions. 'Women of the noblest and wealthiest families, surrounded by the seductive allurements of worldly pleasure, renounced them all. Undismayed by severe edicts against the new religion, they appeared before the magistrates, and by pronouncing the simple words, "I am a Christian," calmly resigned themselves to imprisonment, ignominy and death.' Could such women have had their minds occupied by the foolish vanity of ornamental apparel? No! Christianity struck at the root of all sin, and consequently we find the early Christians could not fight, or swear, or wear costly clothing. Cave, in his work entitled 'Primitive Christianity,' has some interesting remarks on this subject, showing that simplicity of dress was not then esteemed an unimportant part of Christianity.

Very soon, however, when the fire of persecution was no longer blazing, pagan customs became interwoven with Christianity. The professors of the religion of a self-denying Lord, whose kingdom was not of this world, began to use the sword, to return railing for railing, to take oaths, to mingle heathen forms and ceremonies with Christian worship, to engraft on the beautiful simplicity of piety, the feasts and observances which were usual at heathen festivals in honor of the gods, and to adorn their persons with rich and ornamental apparel. And now if we look at Christendom, there is scarcely a vestige of that religion, which the Redeemer of men came to promulgate. The Christian world is much in the situation of the Jewish nation, when the babe of Bethlehem was born, full of outside observances, which they substitute for mercy and love, for self-denial and good works, rigid in the performance of religious duties, but ready, if the Lord Jesus came amongst them and judged them by their fruits, as he did the Pharisees formerly, to crucify him as a slanderer. Indeed, I believe the remark of a late author is perfectly correct:

'Strange as it may seem, yet I do not hesitate to declare my belief that it is easier to make Pagan nations Christians, than to reform Christian communities and fashion them

anew, after the pure and simple standard of the gospel.
Cast your eye over Christian countries, and see what a multitude of causes combine to resist and impair the influence
of Christian institutions. Behold the conformity of Christians to the world, in its prodigal pleasures and frivolous
amusements, in its corrupt opinions and sentiments, of false
honor. Behold the wide spread ignorance and degrading
superstition; the power of prejudice and the authority of
custom; the unchristian character of our systems of education; and the dread of the frowns and ridicule of the world,
and we discover at once a host of more formidable enemies
to the progress of *true religion* in Christian, than in heathen
lands.'

But I must proceed to examine what is the
state of professing Christendom, as regards the
subject of this letter. A few words will suffice.
The habits and employments of fashionable
circles are nearly the same throughout Christian communities. The fashion of dress, which
varies more rapidly than the changing seasons,
is still, as it has been from time immemorial,
an all-absorbing object of interest. The simple
cobbler of Agawam, who wrote in Massachusetts as early as 1647, speaking of women,
says,

' It is no marvel they wear drailes on the hinder part of
their heads, having nothing, as it seems, in the fore part,
but a few squirrels' brains to help them frisk from one fashion
to another.'

It must, however, be conceded, that although
there are too many women who merit this severe
reprehension, there is a numerous class whose
improvement of mind and devotion to the cause
of humanity justly entitle them to our respect
and admiration. One of the most striking
characteristics of modern times, is the tendency
toward a universal dissemination of knowledge
in all Protestant communities. But the character of woman has been elevated more by par-

ticipating in the great moral enterprises of the day, than by anything else. It would astonish us if we could see at a glance all the labor, the patience, the industry, the fortitude which woman has exhibited, in carrying on the causes of Moral Reform, Anti-Slavery, &c. Still, even these noble and ennobling pursuits have not destroyed personal vanity. Many of those who are engaged in these great and glorious reformations, watch with eager interest, the ever varying freaks of the goddess of fashion, and are not exceeded by the butterflies of the ball-room in their love of curls, artificial flowers, embroidery and gay apparel. Many a woman will ply her needle with ceaseless industry, to obtain money to forward a favorite benevolent scheme, while at the same time she will expend on useless articles of dress, more than treble the sum which she procures by the employment of her needle, and which she might throw into the Lord's treasury, and leave herself leisure to cultivate her mind, and to mingle among the poor and the afflicted more than she can possibly do now.

I feel exceedingly solicitous to draw the attention of my sisters to this subject. I know that it is called trifling, and much is said about dressing fashionably, and elegantly, and becomingly, without thinking about it. This I do not believe can be done. If we indulge our fancy in the chameleon caprices of fashion, or in wearing ornamental and extravagant apparel, the mind must be in no small degree engaged in the gratification of personal vanity.

Lest any one may suppose from my being a Quaker, that I should like to see a uniform dress adopted, I will say, that I have no partiality for their peculiar costume, except so far as I find it simple and convenient; and I have not the remotest desire to see it worn, where one more commodious can be substituted. But I do believe one of the chief obstacles in the way of woman's elevation to the same platform of human rights, and moral dignity, and intellectual improvement, with her brother, on which God placed her, and where he designed her to act her part as an immortal creature, is her love of dress. 'It has been observed,' says Scott, 'that foppery and extravagance as to dress *in men* are most emphatically condemned by the apostle's silence on the subject, for this intimated that surely *they* could be under no temptation to such a childish vanity.' But even those men who are superior to such a childish vanity in themselves, are, nevertheless, ever ready to encourage it in women. They know that so long as we submit to be dressed like dolls, we never can rise to the stations of duty and usefulness from which they desire to exclude us; and they are willing to grant us paltry indulgences, which forward their own design of keeping us out of our appropriate sphere, while they deprive us of essential rights.

To me it appears beneath the dignity of woman to bedeck herself in gewgaws and trinkets, in ribbons and laces, to gratify the eye of man. I believe, furthermore, that we owe a solemn duty to the poor. Many a woman, in what is called humble life, spends nearly all her earnings in dress, because she wants to be as well attired as her employer. It is often argued that, as the birds and the flowers are gaily adorned by nature's hand, there can be no sin in woman's ornamenting her person. My reply is, God created me neither a bird nor a flower; and I aspire to something more than a resemblance to them. Besides, the gaudy colors in which birds and flowers are arrayed, create in them no feelings of vanity; but as human beings, we are susceptible of these passions, which are nurtured and strengthened by such adornments. ' Well,' I am often asked, ' where is the limitation?' This it is not my business to decide. Every woman, as Judson remarks, can best settle this on her knees before God. He has commanded her not to be conformed to this world, but to be transformed by the renewing of her mind, that she may know what is the good and acceptable and perfect will of God. He made the dress of the Jewish women the subject of special denunciation by his prophet—Is. 3. 16—26; yet the chains and the bracelets, the rings and the ear-rings, and the changeable suits of apparel, are still worn by Christian women. He has commanded them, through his apostles, not to adorn themselves with broidered hair, or gold, or pearls, or costly array. Not to let their adorning be the ' outward adorning of plaiting the hair, or of wearing of gold, or of putting on of apparel, but let it be the hidden man of the heart, in that which is not corruptible, even the ornament of a meek and quiet spirit, which is in the sight of God of great price; ' yet we disregard these solemn admonitions. May we not form some correct estimate of dress, by asking ourselves how we should feel, if we saw ministers of the gospel rise to address an audience with ear-rings dangling from their ears, glittering rings on their fingers, and a wreath of artificial flowers on their brow, and the rest of their apparel in keeping? If it would be wrong for a minister, it is wrong for every professing Christian. God makes no distinction between the moral and religious duties of ministers and people. We are bound to be 'a chosen generation, a royal priesthood, a peculiar people, a holy nation; that we should show forth the praises of him who hath called us out of darkness into his marvellous light.'

Thine in the bonds of womanhood,

SARAH M. GRIMKE.

LETTER XII.

Concord, 9*th Mo.*, 6*th*, 1837.

My Dear Sister,—There are few things which present greater obstacles to the improvement and elevation of woman to her appropriate sphere of usefulness and duty, than the laws which have been enacted to destroy her independence, and crush her individuality; laws which, although they are framed for her government, she has had no voice in establishing, and which rob her of some of her *essential rights*. Woman has no political existence. With the single exception of presenting a petition to the legislative body, she is a cipher in the nation; or, if not actually so in representative governments, she is only counted, like the slaves of the South, to swell the number of law-makers who form decrees for her government, with little reference to her benefit, except so far as her good may promote their own. I am not sufficiently acquainted with the laws respecting women on the continent of Europe, to say anything about them. But Prof. Follen, in his essay on 'The Cause of Freedom in our Country,' says, 'Woman, though fully possessed of that rational and moral nature which is the foundation of all rights, enjoys amongst us fewer legal rights than under the civil law of continental Europe.' I shall confine myself to the laws of our country. These laws bear with peculiar rigor on married women. Blackstone, in the chapter entitled 'Of husband and wife,' says :—

'By marriage, the husband and wife are one person in law; that is, *the very being, or legal existence of the woman* is suspended during the marriage, or at least is incorporated and consolidated into that of the husband under whose wing, protection and cover she performs everything.' 'For this reason, a man cannot grant anything to his wife, or enter into covenant with her; for the grant would be to suppose her separate existence, and to covenant with her would be to covenant with himself; and therefore it is also generally true, that all compacts made between husband and wife when single, are voided by the intermarriage. A woman indeed may be attorney for her husband, but that implies no separation from, but is rather a representation of, her love.'

Here now, the very being of a woman, like that of a slave, is absorbed in her master. All contracts made with her, like those made with slaves by their owners, are a mere nullity. Our kind defenders have legislated away almost all our legal rights, and in the true spirit of such injustice and oppression, have kept us in ignorance of those very laws by which we are governed. They have persuaded us, that we have no right to investigate the laws, and that, if we did, we could not comprehend them; they alone are capable of understanding the mysteries of Blackstone, &c. But they are not backward to make us feel the practical operation of their power over our actions.

'The husband is bound to provide his wife with necessaries by law, as much as himself; and if she contracts debts for them, he is obliged to pay for them; but for anything besides necessaries, he is not chargeable.'

Yet a man may spend the property he has acquired by marriage at the ale-house, the gambling table, or in any other way that he pleases. Many instances of this kind have come to my knowledge; and women, who have brought their husbands handsome fortunes, have been left, in consequence of the wasteful and dissolute habits of their husbands, in straitened circumstances, and compelled to toil for the support of their families.

'If the wife be indebted before marriage, the husband is bound afterwards to pay the debt; for he has adopted her and her circumstances together.'

The wife's property is, I believe, equally liable for her husband's debts contracted before marriage.

'If the wife be injured in her person or property, she can bring no action for redress without her husband's concurrence, and his name as well as her own : neither can she be sued, without making her husband a defendant.'

This law that 'a wife can bring no action,' &c., is similar to the law respecting slaves. 'A slave cannot bring a suit against his master, or any other person, for an injury—his master, must bring it.' So if any damages are recovered for an injury committed on a wife, the husband pockets it; in the case of the slave, the master does the same.

'In criminal prosecutions, the wife may be indicted and punished separately, unless there be evidence of coercion from the fact that the offence was committed in the presence, or by the command of her husband. A wife is excused from punishment for theft committed in the presence, or by the command of her husband.'

It would be difficult to frame a law better calculated to destroy the responsibility of woman as a moral being, or a free agent. Her husband is supposed to possess unlimited control over her; and if she can offer the flimsy excuse that he bade her steal, she may break the eighth commandment with impunity, as far as human laws are concerned.

'Our law, in general, considers man and wife as one person; yet there are some instances in which she is separately considered, as inferior to him and acting by his compulsion. Therefore, all deeds executed, and acts done by her during her coverture (i. e. marriage,) are void, except it be a fine, or like matter of record, in which case she must be solely and secretly examined, to learn if her act be voluntary.'

Such a law speaks volumes of the abuse of that power which men have vested in their own hands. Still the private examination of a wife, to know whether she accedes to the disposition of property made by her husband is, in most cases, a mere form; a wife dares not do what will be disagreeable to one who is, in his own estimation, her superior, and who makes her feel, in the privacy of domestic life, that she has thwarted him. With respect to the nullity of deeds or acts done by a wife, I will mention one circumstance. A respectable woman borrowed of a female friend a sum of money to relieve her son from some distressing pecuniary embarrassment. Her husband was from home, and she assured the lender, that as soon as he returned, he would gratefully discharge the debt. She gave her note, and the lender, entirely ignorant of the law that a man is not obliged to discharge such a debt, actually borrowed the money, and lent it to the distressed and weeping mother. The father returned home, refused to pay the debt, and the person who had loaned the money was obliged to pay both principal and interest to the friend who lent it to her. Women should certainly know the laws by

which they are governed, and from which they
frequently suffer; yet they are kept in ignorance, nearly as profound, of their legal rights,
and of the legislative enactments which are
to regulate their actions, as slaves.

'The husband, by the old law, might give his wife moderate correction, as he is to answer for her misbehavior.
The law thought it reasonable to entrust him with this
power of restraining her by domestic chastisement. The
courts of law will still permit a husband to restrain a wife
of her liberty, in case of any gross misbehavior.'

What a mortifying proof this law affords, of
the estimation in which woman is held! She
is placed completely in the hands of a being
subject like herself to the outbursts of passion,
and therefore unworthy to be trusted with power. Perhaps I may be told respecting this law,
that it is a dead letter, as I am sometimes told
about the slave laws; but this is not true in
either case. The slaveholder does kill his slave
by moderate correction, as the law allows; and
many a husband, among the poor, exercises the
right given him by the law, of degrading
woman by personal chastisement. And among
the higher ranks, if actual imprisonment is not
resorted to, women are not unfrequently restrained of the liberty of going to places of worship
by irreligious husbands, and of doing many
other things about which, as moral and responsible beings, *they* should be the *sole* judges.
Such laws remind me of the reply of some little girls at a children's meeting held recently at
Ipswich. The lecturer told them that God had
created four orders of beings with which he
had made us acquainted through the Bible.
The first was angels, the second was man,

the third beasts; and now, children, what is the
fourth? After a pause, several girls replied,
' WOMEN.'

' A woman's personal property by marriage becomes absolutely der husband's, which, at his death, he may leave
entirely away from her.'

And farther, all the avails of her labor are
absolutely in the power of her husband. All
that she acquires by her industry is his; so
that she cannot, with her own honest earnings,
become the legal purchaser of any property.
If she expends her money for articles of furni-
ture, to contribute to the comfort of her family,
they are liable to be seized for her husband's
debts: and I know an instance of a woman,
who by labor and economy had scraped together a little maintenance for herself and a do-little
husband, who was left, at his death, by virtue
of his last will and testament, to be supported
by charity. I knew another woman, who by
great industry had acquired a little money which
she deposited in a bank for safe keeping. She
had saved this pittance whilst able to work, in
hopes that when age or sickness disqualified her
for exertion, she might have something to render life comfortable, without being a burden to
her friends. Her husband, a worthless, idle
man, discovered this hid treasure, drew her little stock from the bank, and expended it all in
extravagance and vicious indulgence. I know
of another woman, who married without the
least idea that she was surrendering her rights
to all her personal property. Accordingly, she
went to the bank as usual to draw her dividends, and the person who paid her the money,
and to whom she was personally known as an

owner of shares in that bank, remarking the change in her signature, withdrew the money, informing her that if she were married, she had no longer a right to draw her dividends without an order from her husband. It appeared that she intended having a little fund for private use, and had not even told her husband that she owned this stock, and she was not a little chagrined, when she found that it was not at her disposal. I think she was wrong to conceal the circumstance. The relation of husband and wife is too near and sacred to admit of secrecy about money matters, unless positive necessity demands it; and I can see no excuse for any woman entering into a marriage engagement with a design to keep her husband ignorant that she was possessed of property. If she was unwilling to give up her property to his disposal, she had infinitely better have remained single.

The laws above cited are not very unlike the slave laws of Louisiana.

‘All that a slave possesses belongs to his master; he possesses nothing of his own, except what his master chooses he should possess.’

‘By the marriage, the husband is absolutely master of the profits of the wife's lands during the coverture, and if he has had a living child, and survives the wife, he retains the whole of those lands, if they are estates of inheritance, during his life; but the wife is entitled only to one third if she survives, out of the husband's estates of inheritance. But this she has, whether she has had a child or not.’ ‘With regard to the property of women, there is taxation without representation; for they pay taxes without having the liberty of voting for representatives.’

And this taxation, without representation, be it remembered, was the cause of our Revolutionary war, a grievance so heavy, that it was thought necessary to purchase exemption from

it at an immense expense of blood and treasure,
yet the daughters of New England, as well as
of all the other States of this free Republic, are
suffering a similar injustice—but for one, I had
rather we should suffer any injustice or oppression, than that my sex should have any voice in
the political affairs of the nation.

The laws I have quoted, are, I believe, the
laws of Massachusetts, and, with few exceptions, of all the States in this Union. 'In
Louisiana and Missouri, and possibly, in some
other southern States, a woman not only has
half her husband's property by right at his
death, but may always be considered as possessed of half his gains during his life; having at all times power to bequeath that amount.'
That the laws which have generally been adopted in the United States, for the government of
women, have been framed almost entirely for
the exclusive benefit of men, and with a design
to oppress women, by depriving them of all
control over their property, is too manifest to be
denied. Some liberal and enlightened men, I
know, regret the existence of these laws; and I
quote with pleasure an extract from Harriet
Martineau's Society in America, as a proof of
the assertion. 'A liberal minded lawyer of
Boston, told me that his advice to testators always is to leave the largest possible amount to
the widow, subject to the condition of her leaving it to the children; but that it is with shame
that he reflects that any woman should owe that
to his professional advice, which the law should
have secured to her as a right.' I have known
a few instances where men have left their whole
property to their wives, when they have died,
leaving only minor children; but I have known

6

more instances of 'the friend and helper of many years, being portioned off like a salaried domestic,' instead of having a comfortable independence secured to her, while the children were amply provided for.

As these abuses do exist, and women suffer intensely from them, our brethren are called upon in this enlightened age, by every sentiment of honor, religion and justice, to repeal these unjust and unequal laws, and restore to woman those rights which they have wrested from her. Such laws approximate too nearly to the laws enacted by slaveholders for the government of their slaves, and must tend to debase and depress the mind of that being, whom God created as a help meet for man, or 'helper like unto himself,' and designed to be his equal and his companion. Until such laws are annulled, woman never can occupy that exalted station for which she was intended by her Maker. And just in proportion as they are practically disregarded, which is the case to some extent, just so far is woman assuming that independence and nobility of character which she ought to exhibit.

The various laws which I have transcribed, leave women very little more liberty, or power, in some respects, than the slave. 'A slave,' says the civil code of Louisiana, 'is one who is in the power of a master, to whom he belongs. He can possess nothing, nor acquire anything, but what must belong to his master.' I do not wish by any means to intimate that the condition of free women can be compared to that of slaves in suffering, or in degradation; still, I believe the laws which deprive married women of their rights and privileges, have a tendency to lessen them in their own estimation as moral and responsible beings, and that their being made by civil law inferior to their husbands, has a debasing and mischievous effect upon them, teaching them practically the fatal lesson to look unto man for protection and indulgence.

Ecclesiastical bodies, I believe, without exception, follow the example of legislative assemblies, in excluding woman from any participation in forming the discipline by which she is governed. The men frame the laws, and, with few exceptions, claim to execute them on both sexes. In ecclesiastical, as well as civil courts, woman is tried and condemned, not by a jury of her peers, but by beings, who regard themselves as her superiors in the scale of creation. Although looked upon as an inferior, when considered as an intellectual being, woman is punished with the same severity as man, when she is guilty of moral offences. Her condition resembles, in some measure, that of the slave, who, while he is denied the advantages of his more enlightened master, is treated with even greater rigor of the law. Hoping that in the various reformations of the day, women may be relieved from some of their legal disabilities, I remain,

Thine in the bonds of womanhood,
SARAH M. GRIMKE.

LETTER XIII.

Brookline, 9th Mo., 1837.

MY DEAR SISTER,—Perhaps some persons may wonder that I should attempt to throw out my views on the important subject of marriage, and may conclude that I am altogether disqualified for the task, because I lack experience. However, I shall not undertake to settle the specific duties of husbands and wives, but only to exhibit opinions based on the word of God, and formed from a little knowledge of human nature, and close observation of the working of generally received notions respecting the dominion of man over woman.

When Jehovah ushered into existence man, created in his own image, he instituted marriage as a part of paradisaical happiness : it was a *divine ordination*, not a civil contract. God established it, and man, except by special permission, has no right to annul it. There can be no doubt that the creation of Eve perfected the happiness of Adam ; hence, our all-wise and merciful Father made her as he made Adam, in his own image after his likeness, crowned her with glory and honor, and placed in her hand, as well as in his, the sceptre of dominion over the whole lower creation. Where there was perfect equality, and the same ability to receive and comprehend divine truth, and to obey divine injunctions, there could be no superiority. If God had placed Eve under the guardianship of Adam, after having endowed her, as richly as him, with moral perceptions, intellectual faculties, and spiritual apprehensions, he would at once have interposed a fallible being between her and her Maker. He could not, in simple consistency with himself, have done this; for the Bible teems with instructions not to put any confidence in man.

The passage on which the generally received opinion, that husbands are invested by divine command with authority over their wives, as I have remarked in a previous letter, is a prediction; and I am confirmed in this belief, because the same language is used to Cain respecting Abel. The text is obscure; but on a comparison of it with subsequent events, it appears to me that it was a prophecy of the dominion which Cain would usurp over his brother, and which issued in the murder of Abel. It could not allude to any thing but physical dominion, because Cain had already exhibited those evil passions which subsequently led him to become an assassin.

I have already shown, that man has exercised the most unlimited and brutal power over woman, in the peculiar character of husband,— a word in most countries synonymous with tyrant. I shall not, therefore, adduce any further proofs of the fulfilment of that prophecy, 'He will rule over thee,' from the history of heathen nations, but just glance at the condition of woman in the relation of wife in Christian countries.

'Previous to the introduction of the religion of Jesus Christ, the state of society was wretchedly diseased. The relation of the sexes to each other had become so gross in its manifested forms, that it was difficult to perceive the pure conservative principle in its inward essence.' Christianity came in, at this juncture, with its hallowed influence, and has without doubt tended to lighten the yoke of bondage, to purify the manners, and give the spiritual in some degree an empire over the animal nature. Still, that state which was designed by God to increase the happiness of woman as well as man, often proves the means of lessening her comfort. and degrading her into the mere machine of another's convenience and pleasure. Woman, instead of being elevated by her union with man, which might be expected from an alliance with a superior being, is in reality lowered. She generally loses her individuality, her independent character, her moral being. She becomes absorbed into him, and henceforth is looked at, and acts through the medium of her husband.

In the wealthy classes of society, and those who are in comfortable circumstances, women are exempt from great corporeal exertion, and are protected by public opinion, and by the genial influence of Christianity, from much physical ill treatment. Still, there is a vast amount of secret suffering endured, from the forced submission of women to the opinions and whims of their husbands. Hence they are frequently driven to use deception, to compass their ends. They are early taught that to appear to yield, is the only way to govern. Miserable sophism! I deprecate such sentiments, as being peculiarly hostile to the dignity of woman. If she submits, let her do it openly, honorably, not to gain her point, but as a matter of Christian duty. But let her beware how she permits her husband to be her conscience-keeper. On all moral and religious subjects, she is bound to think and to act for herself. Where confidence and love exist, a wife will naturally converse with her husband as with her dearest friend, on all that interests her heart, and there will be a perfectly free interchange of sentiment; but *she is no more bound to be governed by his judgment*, than he is by hers. They are standing on the same platform of human rights, are equally under the government of God, and accountable to him, and him alone.

I have sometimes been astonished and grieved at the servitude of women, and at the little idea many of them seem to have of their own moral existence and responsibilities. A woman who is asked to sign a petition for the abolition of slavery in the District of Columbia, or to join a society for the purpose of carrying forward the annihilation of American slavery, or any other great reformation, not unfrequently replies, ' My husband does not approve of it.' She merges her rights and her duties in her husband, and thus virtually chooses him for a savior and a king, and rejects Christ as her Ruler and Redeemer. I know some women are very glad of so convenient a pretext to shield themselves from the performance of duty ; but there are others, who, under a mistaken view of their obligations as wives, submit conscientiously to this species of oppression, and go mourning on their way, for want of that holy fortitude, which would enable them to fulfil their duties as moral and responsible beings, without reference to poor fallen man. O that woman may arise in her dignity as an immortal creature, and speak, think and act as unto God, and not unto man!

There is, perhaps, less bondage of mind among the poorer classes, because their sphere of duty is more contracted, and they are deprived of the means of intellectual culture, and of the opportunity of exercising their judgment, on many moral subjects of deep interest and of vital importance. Authority is called into exercise by resistance, and hence there will be mental bondage only in proportion as the faculties of mind are evolved, and woman feels herself as a rational and intelligent being, on a footing with man. But women, among the lowest classes of society, so far as my observation has extended, suffer intensely from the brutality of their husbands. Duty as well as inclination has led me, for many years, into the abodes of poverty and sorrow, and I have been amazed at the treatment which women receive at the hands of those, who arrogate to themselves the epithet of *protectors*. Brute force, the law of violence, rules to a great extent in the poor man's domicil; and woman is little more than his drudge. They are less under the supervision of public opinion, less under the restraints of education, and unaided or unbiased by the refinements of polished society. Religion, wherever it exists, supplies the place of all these; but the real cause of woman's degradation and suffering in married life is to be found in the erroneous notion of her inferiority to man; and never will she be rightly regarded by herself, or others, until this opinion, so derogatory to the wisdom and mercy of God, is exploded, and woman arises in all the majesty of her womanhood, to claim those rights which are inseparable from her existence as an immortal, intelligent and responsible being.

Independent of the fact, that Jehovah could not, consistently with his character as the King, the Lawgiver, and the Judge of his people, give the reins of government over woman into the hands of man, I find that all his commands, all his moral laws, are addressed to women as well as to men. When he assembled Israel at the foot of Mount Sinai, to issue his commandments, we may reasonably suppose he gave all the precepts, which he considered necessary for the government of moral beings. Hence we find that God says,—'Honor thy father and thy mother,' and he enforces this command by severe penalties upon those who transgress it: 'He that smiteth his father, or his mother, shall surely be put to death'—'He that curseth his father, or his mother, shall surely be put to death'—Ex. 21: 15, 17. But in the decalogue, there is no direction given to women to obey their husbands: both are commanded to have no other God but Jehovah, and not to bow down, or serve any other. When the Lord Jesus delivered his sermon on the Mount, full of the practical precepts of religion, he did not issue any command to wives to obey their husbands. When he is speaking on the subject of divorce, Mark 16: 11, 12, he places men and women on the same gound. And the Apostle,

1st Cor. 7 : 12, 13, speaking of the duties of the Corinthian wives and husbands, who had embraced Christianity, to their unconverted partners, points out the same path to both, although our translators have made a distinction. ' Let him not put her away,' 12—' Let her not leave him,' 13—is precisely the same in the original. If man is constituted the governor of woman, he must be her God ; and the sentiment expressed to me lately, by a married man, is perfectly correct : ' In my opinion,' said he, ' the greatest excellence to which a married woman can attain, is to worship her husband.' He was a professor of religion—his wife a lovely and intelligent woman. He only spoke out what thousands think and act. Women are indebted to Milton for giving to this false notion, confirmation strong as proof of holy writ.' His Eve is embellished with every personal grace, to gratify the eye of her admiring husband ; but he seems to have furnished the mother of mankind with just intelligence enough to comprehend her supposed inferiority to Adam, and to yield unresisting submission to her lord and master. Milton puts into Eve's mouth the following address to Adam :

> ' My author and disposer, what thou bidst,
> Unargued I obey ; so God ordains—
> God is thy law, thou mine : to know no more,
> Is woman's happiest knowledge and her praise.'

This much admired sentimental nonsense is fraught with absurdity and wickedness. If it were true, the commandment of Jehovah should have run thus : Man shall have no other gods before ME, and woman shall have no other gods before MAN.

The principal support of the dogma of woman's inferiority, and consequent submission to her husband, is found in some passages of Paul's epistles. I shall proceed to examine those passages, premising 1st, that the antiquity of the opinions based on the false construction of those passages, has no weight with me: they are the opinions of interested judges, and I have no particular reverence for them, *merely* because they have been regarded with veneration from generation to generation. So far from this being the case, I examine any opinions of centuries standing, with as much freedom, and investigate them with as much care, as if they were of yesterday. I was educated to think for myself, and it is a privilege I shall always claim to exercise. 2d. Notwithstanding my full belief, that the apostle Paul's testimony, respecting himself, is true, 'I was not a whit behind the chiefest of the apostles,' yet I believe his mind was under the influence of Jewish prejudices respecting women, just as Peter's and the apostles were about the uncleanness of the Gentiles. 'The Jews,' says Clarke, 'would not suffer a woman to read in the synagogue, although a servant, or even a child, had this permission.' When I see Paul shaving his head for a vow, and offering sacrifices, and circumcising Timothy, to accommodate himself to the prepossessions of his countrymen, I do not conceive that I derogate in the least from his character as an inspired apostle, to suppose that he may have been imbued with the prevalent prejudices against women.

In 1st Cor. 11: 3, after praising the Corinthian converts, because they kept the 'ordinances,' or 'traditions,' as the margin reads, the apostle says, 'I would have you know, that the head of every man is Christ, and the head of the woman is the man; and the head of Christ is God.' Eph. 5: 23, is a parallel passage. 'For the husband is the head of the wife, even as Christ is the head of the Church.' The apostle closes his remarks on this subject, by observing, 'This is a great mystery, but I speak concerning Christ and the Church.' I shall pass over this with simply remarking, that God and Christ are one. 'I and my Father are one,' and there can be no inferiority where there is no divisibility. The commentaries on this and similar texts, afford a striking illustration of the ideas which men entertain of their own superiority, I shall subjoin Henry's remarks on 1st Cor. 11: 5, as a specimen: 'To understand this text, it must be observed, that it was a signification either of shame, or subjection, for persons to be veiled, or covered in Eastern countries; contrary to the custom of ours, where the being bare-headed betokens subjection, and being covered superiority and dominion; and this will help us the better to understand the reason on which he grounds his reprehension, 'Every man praying, &c. dishonoreth his head,' i. e. Christ, the head of every man, by appearing in a habit unsuitable to the rank in which God had placed him. The woman, on the other hand, that prays, &c. dishonoreth her head, i. e. the man. She appears in the dress of her *superior*, and throws off the token of her subjection; she might with equal decency cut her hair short, or cut it off, the common dress of the man in that age. Another reason against this conduct was, that the man is the image and glory of God, the representa-

tive of that glorious dominion and headship
which God has over the world. It is the man
who is set at the head of this lower creation,
and therein bears the resemblance of God.
The woman, on the other hand, is the glory of
the man: she is his representative. Not but she
has dominion over the inferior creatures, and
she is a partaker of human nature, and so far is
God's representative too, but it is at second
hand. She is the image of God, inasmuch as
she is the image of the man. The man was
first made, and made head of the creation here
below, and therein the image of the divine dominion; and the woman was made out of the
man, and shone with a *reflection of his glory*,
being made superior to the other creatures here
below, but in subjection to her husband, and de-
riving that *honor from him*, out of whom she
was made. The woman was made for the man
to be his help meet, and not the man for the
woman. She was, naturally, therefore, made
subject to him, because made for him, for HIS
USE AND HELP AND COMFORT.'

We see in the above quotation, what degrading views even good men entertain of women.
Pity the Psalmist had not thrown a little light
on this subject, when he was paraphrasing the
account of man's creation. 'Thou hast made
him a little lower than the angels, and hast
crowned him with glory and honor. Thou
madest him to have dominion over the works of
thy hands; thou hast put all things under his
feet.' Surely if woman had been placed below
man, and was to shine only by a lustre borrowed from him, we should have some clear evidence of it in the sacred volume. Henry puts
her exactly on a level with the beasts; they

were made for the use, help and comfort of man ; and according to this commentator, this was the whole end and design of the creation of woman. The idea that man, as man is superior to woman, involves an absurdity so gross, that I really wonder how any man of reflection can receive it as of divine origin ; and I can only account for it, by that passion for supremacy, which characterizes man as a corrupt and fallen creature. If it be true that he is more excellent than she, as man, independent of his moral and intellectual powers, then every man is superior by virtue of his manship, to every woman. The man who sinks his moral capacities and spiritual powers in his sensual appetites, is still, as a man, simply by the conformation of his body, a more dignified being, than the woman whose intellectual powers are highly cultivated, and whose approximation to the character of Jesus Christ is exhibited in a blameless life and conversation.

But it is strenuously urged by those, who are anxious to maintain their usurped authority, that wives are, in various passages of the New Testament, commanded to obey their husbands. Let us examine these texts.

Eph. 5, 22. 'Wives, submit yourselves unto your own husbands as unto the Lord.' ' As the church is subject unto Christ, so let the wives be to their own husbands in every thing.'

Col. 3, 18. Wives, submit yourselves unto your own husbands, as it is fit in the Lord.'

1st Pet. 3, 2. 'Likewise ye wives, be in subjection to your own husbands; that if any obey not the word, they may also without the word be won by the conversation of the wives.'

Accompanying all these directions to wives, are commands to husbands.

Eph. 5, 25. 'Husbands, love your wives even as Christ loved the Church, and gave himself for it.' 'So ought men to love their wives as their own bodies. He that loveth his wife, loveth himself.'

Col. 3, 19. 'Husbands, love your wives, and be not bitter against them.'

1st Pet. 3, 7. 'Likewise ye husbands, dwell with them according to knowledge, giving honor unto the wife as unto the weaker vessel, and as being heirs together of the grace of life.'

I may just remark, in relation to the expression 'weaker vessel,' that the word in the original has no reference to intellect : it refers to physical weakness merely.

The apostles were writing to Christian converts, and laying down rules for their conduct towards their unconverted consorts. It no doubt frequently happened, that a husband or a wife would embrace Christianity, while their companions clung to heathenism, and husbands might be tempted to dislike and despise those, who pertinaciously adhered to their pagan superstitions. And wives who, when they were pagans, submitted as a matter of course to their heathen husbands, might be tempted knowing that they were superior as moral and religious characters, to assert that superiority, by paying less deference to them than heretofore. Let us examine the context of these passages, and see what are the grounds of the directions here given to husbands and wives. The whole epistle to the Ephesians breathes a spirit of love. The apostle beseeches the converts to walk worthy of the vocation wherewith they are called, with all lowliness and meekness, with long suffering, forbearing one another in love. The verse preceding 5, 22, is 'SUBMITTING YOURSELVES ONE TO ANOTHER IN THE FEAR OF GOD.' Colossians 3, from

11 to 17, contains similar injunctions. The 17th verse says, 'Whatsoever ye do in word, or in deed, do all in the name of the Lord Jesus.' Peter, after drawing a most touching picture of Christ's sufferings for us, and reminding the Christians, that he had left us an example that we should follow his steps, 'who did no sin, neither was guile found in his mouth,' exhorts wives to be in subjection, &c.

From an attentive consideration of these passages, and of those in which the same words 'submit,' 'subjection,' are used, I cannot but believe that the apostles designed to recommend to wives, as they did to subjects and to servants, to carry out the holy principle laid down by Jesus Christ, 'Resist not evil.' And this without in the least acknowledging the right of the governors, masters, or husbands, to exercise the authority they claimed. The recognition of the existence of evils does not involve approbation of them. God tells the Israelites, he gave them a king in his wrath, but nevertheless as they chose to have a king, he laid down directions for the conduct of that king, and had him anointed to reign over them. According to the generally received meaning of the passages I have quoted, they directly contravene the laws of God, as given in various parts of the Bible. Now I must understand the sacred Scriptures as harmonizing with themselves, or I cannot receive them as the word of God. The commentators on these passages exalt man to the station of a Deity in relation to woman. Clarke says, 'As the Lord Christ is the head, or governor of the church, and the head of the man, so is the man the head, or governor of the woman. This is God's ordinance, and should not be transgressed. 'As unto the Lord.' The word church seems necessarily to be understood here: that is, act under the authority of your husbands, as the church acts under the authority of Christ. As the church submits to the Lord, so let wives submit to their husbands.' Henry goes even further—'For the husband is the head of the wife. The metaphor is taken from the head in the natural body, which being the seat of reason, of wisdom and of knowledge, and the fountain of sense and motion, is more excellent than the rest of the body.' Now if God ordained man the governor of woman, he must be able to save her, and to answer in her stead for all those sins which she commits by his direction. Awful responsibility. Do husbands feel able and willing to bear it? And what becomes of the solemn affirmation of Jehovah? 'Hear this, all ye people, give ear all ye inhabitants of the world, both low and high, rich and poor.' 'None can by any means redeem his brother, or give to God a ransom for him, for the redemption of the soul is precious, and man cannot accomplish it.'—*French Bible.*

Thine in the bonds of womanhood,

SARAH M. GRIMKE.

7

LETTER XIV.

Brookline, 9th Mo. 1837.

My Dear Sister,—According to the principle which I have laid down, that man and woman were created equal, and endowed by their beneficent Creator with the same intellectual powers and the same moral responsibilities, and that consequently whatever is *morally* right for a man to do, is *morally* right for a woman to do, it follows as a necessary corollary, that if it is the duty of man to preach the unsearchable riches of Christ, it is the duty also of woman.

I am aware, that I have the prejudices of education and custom to combat, both in my own and the other sex, as well as ' the traditions of men,' which are taught for the commandments of God. I feel that I have no sectarian views to advance ; for although among the Quakers, Methodists, and Christians, women are permitted to preach the glad tidings of peace and salvation, yet I know of no religious body, who entertain the Scripture doctrine of the perfect equality of man and woman, which is the fundamental principle of my argument in favor of the ministry of women. I wish simply to throw my views before thee. If they are based on the immutable foundation of truth, they cannot be overthrown by unkind insinuations, bitter sarcasms, unchristian imputations, or contemptuous ridicule. These are weapons which are unworthy of a good cause. If I am mistaken, as truth only can prevail, my supposed errors will soon vanish before her beams; but I am persuaded that woman is not filling the high and holy station which God allotted to her, and that in consequence of her having been driven from her 'appropriate sphere,' both herself and her brethren have suffered an infinity of evils.

Before I proceed to prove, that woman is bound to preach the gospel, I will examine the ministry under the Old Testament dispensation. Those who were called to this office were known under various names. Enoch, who prophesied, is designated as walking with God. Noah is called a preacher of righteousness. They were denominated men of God, seers, prophets, but they all had the same great work to perform, viz. to turn sinners from the error of their ways. This ministry existed previous to the institution of the Jewish priesthood, and continued after its abolition. *It has nothing to do with the priesthood.* It was rarely, as far as the Bible informs us, exercised by those of the tribe of Levi, and was common to all the people, women as well as men. It differed essentially from the priesthood, because there was no compensation received for calling the people to repentance. Such a thing as paying a prophet for preaching the truth of God is not even mentioned. They were called of Jehovah to go forth in his name, one from his plough, another from gathering of sycamore fruit, &c. &c. Let us for a moment imagine Jeremiah, when God says to him, 'Gird up thy loins, and arise and speak unto the people all that I command thee,' replying to Jehovah, 'I will preach repentance to the people, if they will give me gold, but if they will not pay me for the truth, then let them perish in their sins.' Now, this is virtually the language of the ministers of the present day; and I believe the secret of the exclusion of women from the ministerial office is, that that office has been converted into one of emolument, of honor, and of power. Any attentive observer cannot fail to perceive, that as far as possible, all such offices are reserved by men for themselves.

The common error that Christian ministers are the successors of the priests, is founded in mistake. In the particular directions given to Moses to consecrate Aaron and his sons to the office of the priesthood, their duties are clearly defined : see Ex. 28th, 29th and 30th chap. There is no commission to Aaron to preach to the people ; his business was to offer sacrifice. Now why were sacrifices instituted? They were types of that one great sacrifice, which in the fulness of time was offered up through the eternal Spirit without spot to God. Christ assumed the office of priest; he 'offered himself,' and by so doing, abolished forever the order of the priesthood, as well as the sacrifices which the priests were ordained to offer.*

* I cannot enter fully into this part of my subject. It is, however, one of great importance, and I recommend those who wish to examine it, to read 'The Book of the Priesthood,' by an English Dissenter, and Beverly's 'View of the Present State of the Visible Church of Christ.' They are both masterly productions.

But it may be inquired, whether the priests were not to teach the people. As far as I can discover from the Bible, they were simply commanded to read the law to the people. There was no other copy that we know of, until the time of the kings, who were to write out a copy for their own use. As it was deposited in the ark, the priests were required, 'When all Israel is come to appear before the Lord thy God in the place which he shall choose, thou shalt read this law before all Israel in their hearing. Gather the people together, men, women, and children, that they may hear,' Deut. 31: 9—33. See also Lev. 10: 11, Deut. 33 : 10, 2d Chr. 17 : 7—9, and numerous other passages. When God is enumerating the means he has used to call his people to repentance, he never, as far as I can discover, speaks of sending his priests to warn them ; but in various passages we find language similar to this : 'Since the day that your fathers came forth out of the land of Egypt unto this day, I have even sent unto you all my servants, the PROPHETS, daily rising up early and sending them. Yet they hearkened not unto me, nor inclined their ear, but hardende their neck ; they did worse than their fathers.' Jer. 7: 25, 26. See also, 25 : 4. 2 Chr. 36 : 15. and parallel passages. God says, Is. 9; 15, 16. ' The prophet that teacheth lies, he is the tail ; for the leaders of this people cause them to err.' The distinction between priests and prophets is evident from their being mentioned as two classes. ' The prophets prophesy falsely, and the priests bear rule by their means,' Jer. 5 : 31. See also, Ch. 2: 8. 8 :1—10. and many others.

That women were called to the prophetic

office, I believe is universally admitted. Miriam,
Deborah and Huldah were prophetesses. The
judgments of the Lord are denounced by Eze-
kiel on false prophetesses, as well as false
prophets. And if Christian ministers are, as I
apprehend, successors of the prophets, and not
of the priests, then of course, women are now
called to that office as well as men, because God
has no where withdrawn from them the privilege of doing what is the great business of
preachers, viz. to point the penitent sinner to
the Redeemer. 'Behold the Lamb of God,
which taketh away the sins of the world.'

It is often triumphantly inquired, why, if
men and women are on an equality, are not
women as conspicuous in the Bible as men ?
I do not intend to assign a reason, but I think
one may readily be found in the fact, that from
the days of Eve to the present time, the aim
of man has been to crush her. He has accomplished this work in various ways; sometimes
by brute force, sometimes by making her sub-
servient to his worst passions, sometimes by
treating her as a doll, and while he excluded
from her mind the light of knowledge, decked
her person with gewgaws and frippery which
he scorned for himself, thus endeavoring to
render her like unto a painted sepulchre.

It is truly marvellous that any woman can
rise above the pressure of circumstances which
combine to crush her. Nothing can strengthen
her to do this in the character of a preacher of
righteousness, but a call from Jehovah himself.
And when the voice of God penetrates the deep
recesses of her heart, and commands her to go
and cry in the ears of the people, she is ready
to exclaim, 'Ah, Lord God, behold I cannot

speak, for I am a woman.' I have known women in different religious societies, who have
felt like the prophet. 'His word was in my
heart as a burning fire shut up in my bones,
and I was weary with forbearing.' But they
have not dared to open their lips, and have endured all the intensity of suffering, produced by
disobedience to God, rather than encounter
heartless ridicule and injurious suspicions. I
rejoice that we have been the oppressed, rather
than the oppressors. God thus prepared his
people for deliverance from outward bondage;
and I hope our sorrows have prepared us to fulfil our high and holy duties, whether public or
private, with humility and meekness; and that
suffering has imparted fortitude to endure trials,
which assuredly await us in the attempt to sun-
der those chains with which man has bound us,
galling to the spirit, though unseen by the eye.

Surely there is nothing either astonishing or
novel in the gifts of the Spirit being bestowed
on woman: nothing astonishing, because there
is no respect of persons with God; the soul of
the woman in his sight is as the soul of the
man, and both are alike capable of the influence
of the Holy Spirit. Nothing novel, because, as
has been already shown, in the sacred records
there are found examples of women, as well as
of men, exercising the gift of prophecy.

We attach to the word prophecy, the exclusive meaning of foretelling future events, but
this is certainly a mistake; for the apostle Paul
defines it to be 'speaking to edification, exhortation and comfort.' And there appears no
possible reason, why women should not do this
as well as men. At the time that the Bible
was translated into English, the meaning of the

word proph'cy, was delivering a message from God, whether it was to predict future events, or to warn the people of the consequences of sin. Governor Winthrop, of Massachusetts, mentions in a letter, that the minister being absent, he went to, —— to prophecy to the people.

Before I proceed to prove that women, under the Christian dispensation, were anointed of the Holy Ghost to preach, or prophecy, I will mention Anna, the (last) prophetess under the Jewish dispensation. ' She departed not from the temple, but served God with fasting and prayers night and day.' And coming into the temple, while Simeon was yet speaking to Mary, with the infant Savior in his arms, 'spake of Christ to all them that looked for redemption in Jerusalem.' Blackwall, a learned English critic, in his work entitled, ' Sacred Classics,' says, in reference to this passage, Luke 2 ; 37—' According to the *original* reading, the sense will be, that the devout Anna, who attended in the temple, both night and day, spoke of the Messiah to all the inhabitants of that city, who constantly worshipped there, and who prepared themselves for the worthy reception of that divine person, whom they expected at this time. And 'tis certain, that other devout Jews, not inhabitants of Jerusalem, frequently repaired to the temple-worship, and might, at this remarkable time, and several others, hear this admirable woman discourse upon the blessed advent of the Redeemer. A various reading has Israel instead of Jerusalem, which expresses that religious Jews, from distant places, came thither to divine offices, and would with high pleasure hear the discourses of this great prophetess, so famed for her extraordinary piety and valuable talents, upon the most important and desirable subject.'

I shall now examine the testimony of the Bible on this point, after the ascension of our Lord, beginning with ...e glorious effusion of the Holy Spirit on the day of Pentecost. I presume it will not be denied, that women, as well as men, were at that time filled with the Holy Ghost, because it is expressly stated, that women were among those who continued in prayer and supplication, waiting for the fulfilment of the promise, that they should be endued with power from on high. 'When the day of Pentecost was fully come, they were ALL with one accord in one place. And there appeared unto them cloven tongues like as of fire, and it sat upon each of them ; and they were all filled with the Holy Ghost, and began to speak with other tongues as the Spirit gave them utterance.' Peter says, in reference to this miracle, ' This is that which was spoken by the prophet Joel. And it shall come to pass in the last days, said God, I will pour out my Spirit upon all flesh ; and your sons and your daughters shall prophesy—and on my servants and on my hand-maidens, I will pour out in those days of my Spirit, and they shall prophesy.' There is not the least intimation that this was a spasmodic influence which was soon to cease. The men and women are classed together ; and if the power to preach the gospel was a supernatural and short-lived impulse in women, then it was equally so in men. But we are told, those were the days of miracles. I grant it; but the men, equally with the women, were the subjects of this marvellous fulfilment of prophecy, and of course, if women

have lost the gift of prophesying, so have men.
We are also gravely told, that if a woman pre-
tends to inspiration, and thereupon grounds the
right to plead the cause of a crucified Redeemer in public, she will be believed when she
shows credentials from heaven, i. e. when she
works a miracle. I reply, if this be necessary
to prove her right to preach the gospel, then I
demand of my brethren to show me their credentials; else I cannot receive their ministry,
by their own showing. John Newton has justly said, that no power but that which created a
world, can make a minister of the gospel; and
man may task his ingenuity to the utmost, to
prove that this power is not exercised on women as well as men. He cannot do it until he
has first disclaimed that simple, but all comprehensive truth, ' in Christ Jesus there is neither
male nor female.'

Women then, according to the Bible, were,
under the New Testament dispensation, as well
as the Old, the recipients of the gift of prophecy. That this is no sectarian view may be
proved by the following extracts. The first I
shall offer is from Stratton's ' Book of the
Priesthood.'

' While they were assembled in the upper room to wait
for the blessing, in number about one hundred and twenty,
they received the miraculous gifts of the Holy Spirit's
grace; they became the channels through which its more
ordinary, but not less saving streams flowed to three thous-
and persons in one day. The whole company of the assembled disciples, male and female, young and old, were all
filled with the Holy Ghost, and began to speak with other
tongues as the Spirit gave them utterance. They all con-
tributed in producing that impression upon the assembled
multitude, which Peter was instrumental in advancing to its
decisive results.'

Scott, in his commentary on this passage, says—

'At the same time, there appeared the form of tongues divided at the tip and resembling fire; one of which rested on each of the whole company.' 'They sat on every one present, as the original determines. At the time of these extraordinary appearances, the whole company were abundantly replenished with the gifts and graces of the Holy Spirit, so that they began to speak with other tongues.'

Henry in his notes confirms this:

'It seems evident to me that not the twelve apostles only, but all the one hundred and twenty disciples were filled with the Holy Ghost alike at this time,—all the seventy disciples, who were apostolical men and employed in the same work, and all the rest too that were to preach the gospel, for it is said expressly, Eph. 4: 8—12: 'When Christ ascended up on high, (which refers to this) he gave gifts unto men.' The all here must refer to the all that were together.'

I need hardly remark that man is a generic term, including both sexes.

Let us now examine whether women actually exercised the office of minister, under the gospel dispensation. Philip had four daughters, who prophesied or preached. Paul calls Priscilla, as well as Aquila, his helpers; or, as in the Greek, his fellow laborers* in Christ Jesus. Divers other passages might be adduced to prove that women continued to be preachers, and that *many* of them filled this dignified station.

We learn also from ecclesiastical history, that female ministers suffered martyrdom in the early ages of the Christian church. In ancient councils, mention is made of deaconesses; and in an edition of the New Testament, printed in 1574, a woman is spoken of as minister of a

* Rom. 16: 3, compare Gr. text of v. 21, 2. Cor. 8: 23; Phil. 2: 25; 1 Thes. 3: 2.

church. The same word, which, in our common translation, is now rendered a servant of the church, in speaking of Phebe, Rom. 16 : 1, is rendered minister, Eph. 6 : 21, when applied to Tychicus. A minister, with whom I had lately the pleasure of conversing, remarked, 'My rule is to expound scripture by scripture, and I cannot deny the ministry of women, because the apostle says, 'help those women who labored with me IN THE GOSPEL.' He certainly meant something more than pouring out tea for him.'

In the 11th Ch. of 1 Cor., Paul gives directions to women and men how they should appear when they prophesy, or pray in public assemblies. It is evident that the design of the apostle, in this and the three succeeding chapters, is to rectify certain abuses which had crept into the Christian church. He therefore admonishes women to pray with their heads covered, because, according to the fashion of that day, it was considered immodest and immoral to do otherwise. He says, 'that were all one as if she were shaven ; ' and shaving the head was a disgraceful punishment that was inflicted on women of bad character.

'These things,' says Scott, ' the apostle stated as decent and proper, but if any of the Corinthian teachers inclined to excite contention about them, he would only add, v. 16, that he and his brethren knew of no such custom as prevailed among them, nor was there any such in the churches of God which had been planted by the other apostles.'

John Locke, whilst engaged in writing his notes on the Epistles of St. Paul, was at a meeting where two women preached. After hearing them, he became convinced of their commission to publish the gospel, and thereupon

altered his notes on the 11th Ch. 1 Cor. in favor of women's preaching.   He says,—

'This about women seeming as difficult a passage as most
in St. Paul's Epistles, I crave leave to premise some few
considerations. It is plain that this covering the head in
women is restrained to some peculiar actions which they
performed in the assembly, expressed by the words praying,
prophesying, which, whatever they signify, must have the
same meaning applied to women in the 5th verse, that they
have when applied to men in the 4th, &c. The next thing
to be considered is, what is here to be understood by praying and prophesying. And that seems to me the performing
of some public action in the assembly, by some one person
which was for that time peculiar to that person, and whilst
it lasted, the rest of the assembly silently assisted. As to
prophesying, the apostle in express words tells us, Ch. 14:
3, 12, that it was speaking in the assembly. The same is
evident as to praying, that the apostle means by it publicly
with an audible voice, ch. 14: 19.'

In a letter to these two women, Rebecca Col-
lier and Rachel Bracken, which accompanied a
little testimony of his regard, he says,

'I admire no converse like that of Christian freedom;
and I fear no bondage like that of pride and prejudice. I
now see that acquaintance by sight cannot reach the height
of enjoyment, which acquaintance by knowledge arrives
unto. Outward hearing may misguide us, but internal knowledge cannot err.' 'Women, indeed, had the honor of first
publishing the resurrection of the God of love—why not
again the resurrection of the spirit of love ? And let all the
disciples of. Christ rejoice therein, as doth your partner,
John Locke.'

See 'The Friend,' a periodical published in
Philadelphia.

Adam Clarke's comment on 1 Cor. 11: 5, is
similar to Locke's :

'Whatever be the meaning of praying and prophesying
in respect to the man, they have precisely the same meaning in respect to the woman. So that some women at least,
as well as some men, might speak to others to edification
and exhortation and comfort. And this kind of prophesying, or teaching, was predicted by Joel 2: 28, and referred

to by Peter; and had there not been such gifts bestowed on women, the prophesy could not have had its fulfilment.

In the autobiography of Adam Clarke, there is an interesting account of his hearing Mary Sewall and another female minister preach, and he acknowledges that such was the power accompanying their ministry, that though he had been prejudiced against women's preaching, he could not but confess that these women were anointed for the office.

But there are certain passages in the Epistles of St. Paul, which seem to be of doubtful interpretation; at which we cannot much marvel, seeing that his brother Peter says, there are some things in them hard to be understood. Most commentators, having their minds preoccupied with the prejudices of education, afford little aid; they rather tend to darken the text by the multitude of words. One of these passages occurs in 1 Cor. 14. I have already remarked, that this chapter, with several of the preceding, was evidently designed to correct abuses which had crept into the assemblies of Christians in Corinth. Hence we find that the men were commanded to be silent, as well as the women, when they were guilty of any thing which deserved reprehension. The apostle says, 'If there be no interpreter, let him keep silence in the church.' The men were doubtless in the practice of speaking in unknown tongues, when there was no interpreter present; and Paul reproves them, because this kind of preaching conveyed no instruction to the people. Again he says, 'If any thing be revealed to another that sitteth by, let the first hold his peace.' We may infer from this, that two men sometimes attempted to speak at the same time, and the apostle rebukes them, and adds, ' Ye may ALL 'prophesy one by one, for God is not the author of confusion, but of peace.' He then proceeds to notice the disorderly conduct of the women, who were guilty of other improprieties. They were probably in the habit of asking questions, on any points of doctrine which they wished more thoroughly explained. This custom was common among the men in the Jewish synagogues, after the pattern of which, the meetings of the early Christians were in all probability conducted. And the Christian women, presuming on the liberty which they enjoyed under the new religion, interrupted the assembly, by asking questions. The apostle disapproved of this, because it disturbed the solemnity of the meeting : he therefore admonishes the women to keep silence in the churches. That the apostle did not allude to preaching is manifest, because he tells them, ' If they will *learn* any thing, let them ask their husbands at home.' Now a person endowed with a gift in the ministry, does not ask questions in the public exercise of that gift, for the purpose of gaining information : she is instructing others. Moreover, the apostle, in closing his remarks on this subject, says, ' Wherefore, brethren, (a generic term, applying equally to men and women,) covet to prophesy, and forbid not to speak with tongues. Let all things be done decently and in order.'

Clarke, on the passage, ' Let women keep silence in the churches,' says :

' This was a Jewish ordinance. Women were not permitted to teach in the assemblies, or even to ask questions The rabbins taught that a woman should know nothing bu the use of her distaff; and the saying of Rabbi Eliezer is worthy of remark and execration: 'Let the words of the law be burned, rather than that they should be delivered by women.'

Are there not many of our Christian brethren, whose hostility to the ministry of women is as bitter as was that of Rabbi Eliezer, and who would rather let souls perish, than that the truths of the gospel should be delivered by women?

'This,' says Clarke, 'was their condition till the time of the gospel, when, according to the prediction of Joel, the Spirit of God was to be poured out on the women as well as the men, that they might prophesy, that is, teach. And that they did prophesy, or teach, is evident from what the apostle says, ch. 11 : 5, where he lays down rules to regulate this part of their conduct while ministering in the church. But does not what the apostle says here, let your women keep silence in the churches, contradict that statement, and show that the words in ch. 11, should be understood in another sense? for here it is expressly said, that they should keep silence in the churches, for it was not permitted to a woman to speak. Both places seem perfectly consistent. It is evident from the context, that the apostle refers here to asking questions, and what we call dictating in the assemblies.'

The other passage on which the opinion, that women are not called to the ministry, is founded, is 1 Tim. 2d ch. The apostle speaks of the duty of prayer and supplication, mentions his own ordination as a preacher, and then adds, 'I will, therefore, that men pray everywhere, lifting up holy hands, without wrath and doubting. In like manner also, that women adorn themselves in modest apparel,' &c. I shall here premise, that as the punctuation and division into chapters and verses is no part of the original arrangement, they cannot determine the sense of a passage. Indeed, every attentive reader of the Bible must observe, that the injudicious separation of sentences often destroys their meaning and their beauty. Joseph John Gurney, whose skill as a biblical critic is well known in England, commenting on this passage, says,

'It is worded in a manner somewhat obscure; but appears to be best construed according to the opinion of various commentators (See Pool's Synopsis) as conveying an injunction, that women as well as men should pray everywhere, lifting up holy hands without wrath and doubting. 1 Tim. 2 : 8, 9. 'I will therefore that men pray everywhere, &c.; likewise also the women in a modest dress.' (Compare 1 Cor. 11 : 5.) 'I would have them adorn themselves with shamefacedness and sobriety.' '

I have no doubt this is the true meaning of the text, and that the translators would never have thought of altering it had they not been under the influence of educational prejudice. The apostle proceeds to exhort the women, who thus publicly made intercession to God, not to adorn themselves with braided hair, or gold, or pearls, or costly array, but (which becometh women professing godliness) with good works.' The word in this verse translated 'professing,' would be more properly rendered preaching godliness, or enjoining piety to the gods, or conducting public worship. After describing the duty of female ministers about their apparel, the apostle proceeds to correct some improprieties which probably prevailed in the Ephesian church, similar to those which he had reproved among the Corinthian converts. He says, 'Let the women LEARN in silence with all subjection; but I suffer not a woman to teach, nor to usurp authority over the man, but to be in silence,' or quietness. Here again it is evident that the women, of whom he was speaking, were admonished to learn in silence, which could not refer to their public ministrations to others. The verb to teach, verse 12, is one of very general import, and may in this place more properly be rendered dictate. It is highly probable that women who had long been in bondage, when set free by Christianity from the restraints imposed upon them by Jewish traditions and heathen customs, run into an extreme in their public assemblies, and interrupted the religious services by frequent interrogations, which they could have had answered as satisfactorily at home.

On a candid examination and comparison of the passages which I have endeavored to explain, viz., 1 Cor. chaps. 11 and 14, and 1 Tim. 2, 8—12. I think we must be compelled to adopt one of two conclusions; either that the apostle grossly contradicts himself on a subject of great practical importance, and that the fulfilment of the prophecy of Joel was a shameful infringement of decency and order; or that the directions given to women, not to speak, or to teach in the congregations, had reference to some local and peculiar customs, which were then common in religious assemblies, and which the apostle thought inconsistent with the purpose for which they were met together. No one, I suppose, will hesitate which of these two conclusions to adopt. The subject is one of vital importance. That it may claim the calm and prayerful attention of Christians, is the desire of

Thine in the bonds of womanhood,

SARAH M. GRIMKE.

LETTER XV.

Uxbridge, 10*th Mo.* 20*th,* 1837.

MY DEAR SISTER,—It is said that 'modern
Jewish women light a lamp every Friday evening, half an hour before sunset, which is the
beginning of their Sabbath, in remembrance of
their original mother, who first extinguished the
lamp of righteousness,—to remind them of their
obligation to rekindle it.' I am one of those
who always admit, to its fullest extent, the pop-
ular charge, that woman brought sin into the
world. I accept it as a powerful reason, why
woman is bound to labor with double diligence,
for the regeneration of that world she has been
instrumental in ruining.

But, although I do not repel the imputation,
I shall notice some passages in the sacred
Scriptures, where this transaction is mentioned,
which prove, I think, the identity and equality
of man and woman, and that there is no difference in their guilt in the view of that God who
searcheth the heart and trieth the reins of the
children of men. In Is. 43 : 27, we find the
following passage—' Thy first father hath sin-

ned, and thy teachers have transgressed against me '—which is synonymous with Rom. 5: 12. ' Wherefore, as by ONE MAN sin entered into the world, and death by sin, &c.' Here man and woman are included under one term, and no distinction is made in their criminality. The circumstances of the fall are again referred to in 2 Cor. 11: 3—' But I fear lest, by any means, as the serpent *beguiled* Eve through his subtility, so your mind should be beguiled from the simplicity that is in Christ.' Again, 1st Tim. 2: 14—' Adam *was not deceived;* but the woman being *deceived,* was in the transgression.' Now, whether the fact, that Eve was beguiled and deceived, is a proof that her crime was of deeper dye than Adam's, who was not deceived, but was fully aware of the consequences of sharing in her transgression, I shall leave the candid reader to determine.

My present object is to show, that, as woman is charged with all the sin that exists in the world, it is her solemn duty to labor for its extinction; and that this she can never do effectually and extensively, until her mind is disenthralled of those shackles which have been riveted upon her by a ' *corrupt public opinion, and a perverted interpretation of the holy Scriptures.*' Woman must feel that she is the equal, and is designed to be the fellow laborer of her brother, or she will be studying to find out the *imaginary* line which separates the sexes, and divides the duties of men and women into two distinct classes, a separation not even hinted at in the Bible, where we are expressly told, ' there is neither male nor female, for ye are all one in Christ Jesus.'

My views on this subject are so much better

embodied in the language of a living author
than I can express them, that I quote the passage entire : ' Woman's rights and man's rights
are *both* contained in the *same* charter, and held
by the *same* tenure. *All rights* spring out of
the *moral* nature : they are both the root and
the offspring of *responsibilities.* The physical
constitution is the mere *instrument* of the *moral* nature ; sex is a mere *incident* of this constitution, a provision necessary to this *form*
of existence ; its *only* design, not to give, nor
to take away, nor in any respect to modify or
even *touch* rights or responsibilities in any sense,
except so far as the peculiar offices of each sex
may afford less or more *opportunity* and ability
for the exercise of rights, and the discharge of
responsibilities ; but merely to continue and enlarge the human department of God's government. Consequently, I know nothing of *man's*
rights, or *woman's* rights ; *human* rights are all
that I recognise. The doctrine, that the *sex of
the body* presides over and administers upon the
rights and responsibilities of the moral, immortal nature, is to my mind a doctrine kindred to
blasphemy, *when seen in its intrinsic nature.*
It breaks up utterly the *relations* of the two na-
tures, and reverses their functions ; exalting the
animal nature into a monarch, and humbling
the moral into a slave ; making the former a
proprietor, and the latter its property.'

To perform our duties, we must comprehend
our rights and responsibilities ; and it is because
we do not understand, that we now fall so far
short in the discharge of our obligations. Un-
accustomed to think for ourselves, and to search
the sacred volume, to see how far we are living
up to the design of Jehovah in our creation, we

have rested satisfied with the sphere marked out for us by man, never detecting the fallacy of that reasoning which forbids woman to exercise some of her noblest faculties, and stamps with the reproach of indelicacy those actions by which women were formerly dignified and exalted in the church.

I should not mention this subject again, if it were not to point out to my sisters what seems to me an irresistible conclusion from the literal interpretation of St. Paul, without reference to the context, and the peculiar circumstances and abuses which drew forth the expressions, 'I suffer not a woman to teach'—'Let your women keep silence in the church,' i. e. congregation. It is manifest, that if the apostle meant what his words imply, when taken in the strictest sense, then women have no right to *teach* Sabbath or day schools, or to open their lips to sing in the assemblies of the people; yet young and delicate women are engaged in all these offices; they are expressly trained to exhibit themselves, and raise their voices to a high pitch in the choirs of our places of worship. I do not intend to sit in judgment on my sisters for doing these things; I only want them to see, that they are as really infringing a *supposed* divine command, by instructing their pupils in the Sabbath or day schools, and by singing in the congregation, as if they were engaged in preaching the unsearchable riches of Christ to a lost and perishing world. Why, then, are we permitted to break this injunction in some points, and so seduously warned not to overstep the bounds set for us by our *brethren* in another? Simply, as I believe, because in the one case we subserve *their* views and *their* interests, and act *in subordination to them;* whilst in the other, we come in contact with their interests, and claim to be on an equality with them in the highest and most important trust ever committed to man, namely, the ministry of the word. It is manifest, that if women were permitted to be ministers of the gospel, as they unquestionably were in the primitive ages of the Christian church, it would interfere materially with the present organized system of spiritual power and ecclesiastical authority, which is now vested solely in the hands of men. It would either show that all the paraphernalia of theological seminaries, &c. &c. to prepare men to become evangelists, is wholly unnecessary, or it would create a necessity for similar institutions in order to prepare women for the same office; and this would be an encroachment on that learning, which our hind brethren have so ungenerously monopolized. I do not ask any one to believe my statements, or adopt my conclusions, because they are mine; but I do earnestly entreat my sisters to lay aside their prejudices, and examine these subjects *for themselves*, regardless of the 'traditions of men,' because they are intimately connected with their duty and their usefulness in the present important crisis.

All who know any thing of the present system of benevolent and religious operations, know that women are performing an important part in them, in *subserviency to men*, who guide our labors, and are often the recipients of those benefits of education we toil to confer, and which we rejoice they can enjoy, although it is their mandate which deprives us of the same advantages. Now, whether our brethren have defrauded us intentionally, or unintentionally, the wrong we suffer is equally the same. For years, they have been spurring us up to the performance of our duties. The immense usefulness and the vast influence of woman have been eulogized and called into exercise, and many a blessing has been lavished upon us, and many a prayer put up for us, because we have labored by day and by night to clothe and feed and educate young men, whilst our own bodies sometimes suffer for want of comfortable garments, and our minds are left in almost utter destitution of that improvement which we are toiling to bestow upon the brethren.

> ' Full many a gem of purest ray serene,
>   The dark unfathomed caves of ocean bear ;
> Full many a flower is born to blush unseen
>   And waste its sweetness on the desert air.'

If the sewing societies, the avails of whose industry are now expended in supporting and educating young men for the ministry, were to withdraw their contributions to these objects, and give them where they are *more needed*, to the advancement of their *own sex* in useful learning, the next generation might furnish sufficient proof, that in intelligence and ability to master the whole circle of sciences, woman is not inferior to man ; and instead of a sensible woman being regarded as she now is, is a lusus naturæ, they would be quite as common as sensible men. I confess, considering the high claim men in this country make to great politeness and deference to women, it does seem a little extraordinary that we should be urged to work for the brethren. I should suppose it would be more in character with ' the generous promptings of chivalry, and the poetry of romantic gallantry,' for which Catherine E.

Beecher gives them credit, for them to form societies to educate their sisters, seeing our inferior capacities require more cultivation to bring
them into use, and qualify us to be helps meet
for them. However, though I think this would
be but a just return for all our past kindnesses
in this way, I should be willing to balance our
accounts, and begin a new course. Henceforth,
let the benefit be reciprocated, or else let each
sex provide for the education of their own poor,
whose talents ought to be rescued from the ob-
livion of ignorance. Sure I am, the young
men who are now benefitted by the handy work
of their sisters, will not be less honorable if they
occupy half their time in earning enough to pay
for their own education, instead of depending
on the industry of women, who not unfrequently deprive themselves of the means of purchas-
ing valuable books which might enlarge their
stock of useful knowledge, and perhaps prove a
blessing to the family by furnishing them with
instructive reading. If the minds of women
were enlightened and improved, the domestic
circle would be more frequently refreshed by
intelligent conversation, a means of edification
now deplorably neglected, for want of that cultivation which these intellectual advantages
would confer.

DUTIES OF WOMEN.

One of the duties which devolve upon women
in the present interesting crisis, is to prepare
themselves for more extensive usefulness, by
making use of those religious and literary privileges and advantages that are within their
reach, if they will only stretch out their hands
and possess them. By doing this, they will

become better acquainted with their rights as moral beings, and with their responsibilities growing out of those rights: they will regard themselves, as they really are, FREE AGENTS, immortal beings, amenable to no tribunal but that of Jehovah, and bound not to submit to any restriction imposed for selfish purposes, or to gratify that love of power which has reigned in the heart of man from Adam down to the present time. In contemplating the great moral reformations of the day, and the part which they are bound to take in them, instead of puzzling themselves with the harassing, because unnecessary inquiry, how far they may go without overstepping the bounds of propriety, which separate male and female duties, they will only inquire, ' Lord, what wilt thou have us to do ? ' They will be enabled to see the simple truth, that God has made no distinction between men and women as moral beings ; that the distinction now so much insisted upon between male and female virtues is as absurd as it is unscriptural, and has been the fruitful source of much mischief—granting to man a license for the exhibition of brute force and conflict on the battle field ; forst ernness, selfishness, and the exercise of irresponsible power in the circle of home— and to woman a permit to rest on an arm of flesh, and to regard modesty and delicacy, and all the kindred virtues, as peculiarly appropriate to her. Now to me it is perfectly clear, that WHATSOEVER IT IS MORALLY RIGHT FOR A MAN TO DO, IT IS MORALLY RIGHT FOR A WOMAN TO DO ; and that confusion must exist in the moral world, until women takes her stand on the same platform with man, and feels that she is clothed by her Maker with the *same rights*, and, of course, that upon her devolve the *same duties*.

It is not my intention, nor indeed do I think it is in my power, to point out the precise duties of women. To him who still teacheth by his Holy Spirit as never man taught, I refer my beloved sisters. There is a vast field of usefulness before them. The signs of the times give portentous evidence, that a day of deep trial is approaching; and I urge them, by every consideration of a Savior's dying love, by the millions of heathen in our midst, by the sufferings of woman in almost every portion of the world, by the fearful ravages which slavery, intemperance, licentiousness and other iniquities are making of the happiness of our fellow creatures, to come to the rescue of a ruined world, and to be found co-workers with Jesus Christ.

> ' Ho ! to the rescue, ho !
>   Up every one that feels—
> 'Tis a sad and fearful cry of woe
>   From a guilty world that steals.
> Hark ! hark ! how the horror rolls,
>   Whence can this anguish be ?
> 'Tis the groan of a trammel'd people's souls,
>   *Now bursting* to be free.'

And here, with all due deference for the office of the ministry, which I believe was established by Jehovah himself, and designed by Him to be the means of spreading light and salvation through a crucified Savior to the ends of the earth, I would entreat my sisters not to *compel* the ministers of the present day to give their names to great moral reformations. The practice of making ministers life members, or officers of societies, when their hearts have not been touched with a live coal from the altar,

and animated with love for the work we are
engaged in, is highly injurious to them, as well
as to the cause. They often satisfy their con-
sciences in this way, without doing anything to
promote the anti-slavery, or temperance, or other reformations; and we please ourselves with
the idea, that we have done something to forward the cause of Christ, when, in effect, we
have been sewing pillows like the false prophetesses of old under the arm-holes of our clerical brethren. Let us treat the ministers with
all tenderness and respect, but let us be careful
how we cherish in their hearts the idea that
they are of more importance to a cause than
other men. I rejoice when they take hold
heartily. I love and honor some ministers with
whom I have been associated in the anti-slavery
ranks, but I do deeply deplore, for the sake of the
cause, the prevalent notion, that the clergy must
be had, either by persuasion or by bribery.
They will not need persuasion or bribery, if
their hearts are with us; if they are not, we
are better without them. It is idle to suppose
that the kingdom of heaven cannot come on
earth, without their co-operation. It is the
Lord's work, and it must go forward with or
without their aid. As well might the converted Jews have despaired of the spread of Christianity, without the co-operation of Scribes and
Pharisees.

Let us keep in mind, that no abolitionism is
of any value, which is not accompanied with
deep, heartfelt repentance ; and that, whenever
a minister sincerely repents of having, either
by his apathy or his efforts, countenanced the
fearful sin of slavery, he will need no induce-
ment to come into our ranks; so far from it, he

will abhor himself in dust and ashes, for his past blindness and indifference to the cause of God's poor and oppressed : and he will regard it as a privilege to be enabled to do something in the cause of human rights. I know the ministry exercise vast power ; but I rejoice in the belief, that the spell is broken which encircled them, and rendered it all but blasphemy to expose their errors and their sins. We are beginning to understand that they are but men, and that their station should not shield them from merited reproof.

I have blushed for my sex when I have heard of their entreating ministers to attend their associations, and open them with prayer. The idea is inconceivable to me, that Christian women can be engaged in doing God's work, and yet cannot ask his blessing on their efforts, except through the lips of a man. I have known a whole town scoured to obtain a minister to open a female meeting, and their refusal to do so spoken of as quite a misfortune. Now, I am not glad that the ministers do wrong; but I am glad that my sisters have been sometimes compelled to act for themselves : it is exactly what they need to strengthen them, and prepare them to act independently. And to say the truth, there is something really ludicrous in seeing a minister enter the meeting, open it with prayer, and then take his departure. However, I only throw out these hints for the consideration of women. I believe there are solemn responsibilities resting upon us, and that in this day of light and knowledge, we cannot plead ignorance of duty. The great moral reformations now on the wheel are only practical Christianity ; and if the ministry is not prepared to labor with us in these righteous causes, let us press forward, and they will follow on to know the Lord.

CONCLUSION.

I have now, my dear sister, completed my series of letters. I am aware, they contain some new views; but I believe they are based on the immutable truths of the Bible. All I ask for them is, the candid and prayerful consideration of Christians. If they strike at some of our bosom sins, our deep-rooted prejudices, our long cherished opinions, let us not condemn them on that account, but investigate them fearlessly and prayerfully, and not shrink from the examination; because, if they are true, they place heavy responsibilities upon women. In throwing them before the public, I have been actuated solely by the belief, that if they are acted upon, they will exalt the character and enlarge the usefulness of my own sex, and contribute greatly to the happiness and virtue of the other. That there is a root of bitterness continually springing up in families and troubling the repose of both men and women, must be manifest to even a superficial observer; and I believe it is the mistaken notion of the inequality of the sexes. As there is an assumption of superiority on the one part, which is not sanctioned by Jehovah, there is an incessant struggle on the other to rise to that degree of dignity, which God designed women to possess in common with men, and to maintain those rights and exercise those privileges which every woman's common sense, apart from the prejudices of education, tells her are inalienable; they are a part of her moral nature, and can only cease when her immortal mind is extinguished.

One word more. I feel that I am calling upon my sex to sacrifice what has been, what is still dear to their hearts, the adulation, the flattery, the attentions of trifling men. I am asking them to repel these insidious enemies whenever they approach them ; to manifest by their conduct, that, although they value highly the society of pious and intelligent men, they have no taste for idle conversation, and for that silly preference which is manifested for their personal accommodation, often at the expense of great inconvenience to their male companions. As an illustration of what I mean, I will state a fact.

I was traveling lately in a stage coach. A gentleman, who was also a passenger, was made sick by riding with his back to the horses. I offered to exchange seats, assuring him it did not affect me at all unpleasantly ; but he was too polite to permit a lady to run the risk of being discommoded. I am sure he meant to be very civil, but I really thought it was a foolish piece of civility. This kind of attention encourages selfishness in woman, and is only accorded as a sort of quietus, in exchange for those *rights* of which we are deprived. Men and women are equally bound to cultivate a spirit of accommodation ; but I exceedingly deprecate her being treated like a spoiled child, and sacrifices made to her selfishness and vanity. In lieu of these flattering but injurious attentions, yielded to her as an inferior, as a mark of benevolence and courtesy, I want my sex to claim nothing from their brethren but what their brethren may justly claim from them,

ın their intercourse as Christians. I am persuaded woman can can do much in this way to
elevate her own character. And that we may
become duly sensible of the dignity of our nature, only a little lower than the angels, and
bring forth fruit to the glory and honor of
Emanuel's name, is the fervent prayer of

Thine in the bonds of womanhood,

SARAH M. GRIMKE.